Gospel Light's

SPECIAL AGENT

CRAFTS FOR KIDS

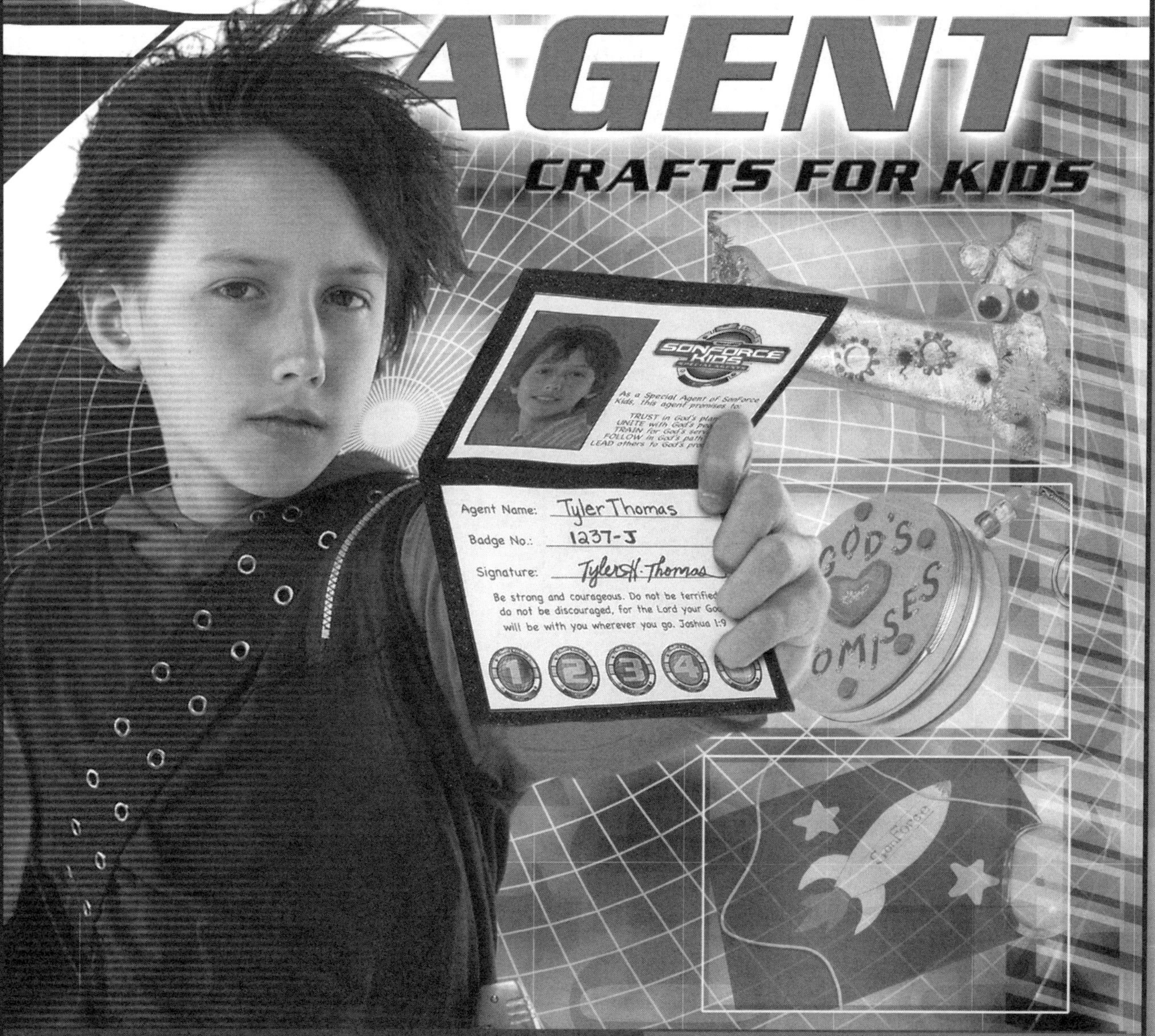

- Fun at Church, Home or School
- Uses Economical, Easy-to-Find Supplies
- **45 Fun Craft Projects** for Children from Preschool to Sixth Grade

REPRODUCIBLE!

HOW TO MAKE CLEAN COPIES FROM THIS BOOK

You may make copies of portions of this book with a clean conscience if

- you (or someone in your organization) are the original purchaser;
- you are using the copies you make for a noncommercial purpose (such as teaching or promoting your ministry) within your church or organization;
- you follow the instructions provided in this book.

However, it is ILLEGAL for you to make copies if

- you are using the material to promote, advertise or sell a product or service other than for ministry fund-raising;
- you are using the material in or on a product for sale; or
- you or your organization are not the original purchaser of this book.

By following these guidelines you help us keep our products affordable.

Thank you,

Gospel Light

Gospel Light Vacation Bible School

Senior Managing Editor, Sheryl Haystead ■ **Senior Editor,** Heather Kempton Wahl ■ **Associate Editor,** Becky Garcia ■ **Contributing Editors,** Suzanne Bass, Antoinette Bell, Carol Eide, Kim Fiano, Teresa Lew, Dianne Rowell ■ **Art Directors,** Lori Hamilton, Samantha Hsu, Lenndy McCullough ■ **Senior Designer,** Carolyn Thomas

Founder, Dr. Henrietta Mears ■ **Publisher,** William T. Greig ■ **Senior Consulting Publisher,** Dr. Elmer L. Towns ■ **Senior Consulting Editor,** Wesley Haystead, M.S.Ed. ■ **Senior Editor, Biblical and Theological Issues,** Bayard Taylor, M.Div.

Contents

Introduction

Special Agent Fun!

Special agent training brings to mind hi-tech gadgets, exciting missions and thrilling adventure. Children get excited when they can use fun and unique gadgets to solve mysteries. The satellite headquarters of the SonForce Kids special agents is the inspiration behind the crafts of this resource book, *Special Agent Crafts for Kids.*

In this hi-tech command center, SonForce agents gather to prepare for their five Daily Missions: Trust! Unite! Train! Follow! Lead! Throughout SonForce Kids VBS, your students will have the opportunity to grow in their understanding of what it means to serve God with courage as they advance from Level 1 to Level 5 agents. Many of these crafts focus on courage demonstrated by the lives of various people from the Bible.

We hope that you and your students will enjoy many fun-filled hours creating these projects from *Special Agent Crafts for Kids*.

Personalize It!

Feel free to alter the craft materials and instructions in this book to suit your children's needs. Consider what materials you have on hand, what materials are available in your area and what materials you can afford to purchase. In some cases, you may be able to substitute materials you already have for the suggested craft supplies.

In addition, don't feel confined to the crafts in a particular age-level section. You may want to adapt a craft for younger or older children by using the simplification or enrichment ideas where provided.

Three Keys to Success

How can you make craft time successful and fun for your children? First, encourage creativity in each child! Remember, the process of creating is more important than the final product. Provide a variety of materials with which children may work. Allow children to make choices on their own. Don't insist that children "stay inside the lines."

Second, choose projects that are appropriate for the skill level of your children. Children can become discouraged when a project is too difficult for them. Finding the right projects for your children will increase the likelihood that they will be successful and satisfied with their finished products.

Finally, show an interest in the unique way each child approaches a project. Affirm the choices he or she has made. Treat each child's final product as a masterpiece!

The comments you give a child today can affect the way he or she views art in the future, so be positive! Being creative is part of being made in the image of God, the ultimate creator!

Craft Symbols

Many of the craft projects in *Special Agent Crafts for Kids* are appropriate for more than one age level. Next to the title of certain projects, you'll find the symbol shown below. This symbol tells which projects are suitable or adaptable for all elementary-age children—first through sixth grades. As you select projects, consider the particular children you are working with. Feel free to use your own ideas to make projects simpler or more challenging, depending on the needs of your children.

In addition, some craft projects in this book require less preparation than others. The symbol shown below tells which projects require minimal preparation.

suitable for all ages

minimal preparation

Crafts with a Message

Many projects in *Special Agent Crafts for Kids* can easily become crafts with a message. Have children create slogans or poetry as part of their projects; or provide photocopies of an appropriate poem, thought or Bible verse for children to attach to their crafts. Below are some examples of ways to use messages to enhance the craft projects in this book.

Conversation

Each craft in this book includes a Conversation section designed to help you enhance craft times with thought-provoking conversation that is age appropriate. The Conversation section for a project may relate to prayer, a Scripture verse or a Bible story. Often Conversation sections will include interesting facts. If your craft program includes large groups of children, share these Conversation suggestions with each helper, who can use them with individuals or small groups.

Be Prepared

If you are planning to use crafts with a child at home, here are some helpful tips:

■ Focus on crafts designed for your child's age, but don't ignore projects for older or younger ages. Elementary-age children enjoy many of the projects geared for preschool and kindergarten children. And younger children are always interested in doing "big kid" things. Just plan on working along with your child, helping with tasks he or she can't handle alone.

■ Start with projects that call for materials you have around the house. Make a list of items you do not have, and plan to gather them in one expedition.

■ If certain materials seem too difficult to obtain, a little thought can usually lead to appropriate substitutions. Often your creative twist ends up being an improvement over the original plan.

If you are planning to lead a group of children in doing craft projects, keep these hints in mind:

■ Choose projects that allow children to work with a variety of materials.

■ Make your project selections far enough in advance to allow time to gather all needed supplies.

■ Make a sample of each project to be sure the directions are fully understood and potential problems can be avoided. **You may want to adapt some projects by simplifying procedures or varying the materials.**

■ Items can often be acquired as donations from people or businesses if you plan ahead and make your needs known. Many churches distribute lists of needed materials to their congregations. Some items can be brought by the children themselves.

■ In making your supply list, distinguish between items that each individual child will need and those that will be shared among a group.

■ Keep in mind that some materials may be shared among more than one age level. To avoid frustration, coordinate with other groups that might be using the same supplies you need so that children can complete their craft projects. Basic supplies that are used in many projects, such as glue, scissors, markers, etc., should be available in every craft room.

Helpful Hints

Using Glue with Young Children

Because preschoolers have difficulty using glue bottles effectively, you may want to purchase glue in large containers (up to one-gallon size) and try one of the following procedures:

a. Pour small amounts of glue into several margarine tubs.

b. Dilute glue by mixing a little water into each container.

c. Children use paintbrushes to spread glue on their projects.

d. When project is completed, place lids on margarine tubs to save glue for future projects.

OR

a. Pour small amounts of glue into several margarine tubs.

b. Give each child a cotton swab.

c. Children dip cotton swabs into the glue and rub glue on projects.

d. When project is completed, place lids on margarine tubs to save glue for future projects.

Cutting with Scissors

When cutting with scissors is required for crafts, remember that some children in your class may be left-handed. It is very difficult for a left-handed person to cut with right-handed scissors. Have available two or three pairs of left-handed scissors. These can be obtained from a school-supply center.

If your craft involves cutting fabric, felt or ribbon, have available several pairs of fabric scissors for older children.

Using Acrylic Paints

Acrylic paints are required for several projects. Our suggestions:

■ Provide smocks or old shirts for your children to wear, as acrylics may stain clothes.

■ Acrylics can be expensive for a large group of children. To make paint go further, dilute it with a small amount of water. Or use house paints thinned with water.

■ Fill shallow containers with soapy water. Clean paintbrushes before switching colors and immediately after finishing project.

Leading a Child to Christ

One of the greatest privileges of serving in VBS is helping children become members of God's family. Pray for the children you teach and ask God to prepare them to understand and receive the good news about Jesus. Ask God to give you the sensitivity and wisdom you need to communicate effectively and to be aware of opportunities that occur naturally.

Because children are easily influenced to follow the group, be cautious about asking for group decisions. Offer opportunities to talk and pray individually with any child who expresses interest in becoming a member of God's family—but without pressure. A good way to guard against coercing a child to respond is to simply ask, "Would you like to hear more about this now or at another time?"

When talking about salvation with children, use words and phrases they understand; never assume they understand a concept just because they can repeat certain words. Avoid symbolic terms ("born again," "ask Jesus to come into your heart," "open your heart," etc.) that will confuse these literal-minded thinkers. (You may also use the evangelism booklet *God Loves You!*)

1. God wants you to become His child. Why do you think He wants you in His family? (See 1 John 3:1.)
2. Every person in the world has done wrong things. The Bible word for doing wrong is "sin." What do you think should happen to us when we sin? (See Romans 6:23.)
3. God loves you so much that He sent His Son to die on the cross to take the punishment for your sin. Because Jesus never sinned, He is the only One who can take the punishment for your sin. (See 1 Corinthians 15:3; 1 John 4:14.)
4. Are you sorry for your sin? Tell God that you are. Do you believe Jesus died for your sin and then rose again? Tell Him that, too. If you tell God you are sorry for your sin and believe that Jesus died to take your sin away, God forgives you. (See 1 John 1:9.)
5. The Bible says that when you believe Jesus is God's Son and is alive today, you receive God's gift of eternal life. This gift makes you a child of God. (See John 3:16.) This means God is with you now and forever.

There is great value in encouraging a child to think and pray about what you have said before responding. Encourage the child who makes a decision to become a Christian to tell his or her parents. Give your pastor and the child's Sunday School teacher(s) his or her name. A child's initial response to Jesus is just the beginning of a lifelong process of growing in the faith, so children who make decisions need to be followed up to help them grow. The discipling booklet *Growing as God's Child* is an effective tool to use.

Age-Level Characteristics

Ages 4 and 5

SonForce Kids prekindergarten and kindergarten materials have been planned for children who are three to six years old with a ratio of one teacher for every four to six children (and can be easily adapted to include two-year-olds with a ratio of one teacher for every four children). Each activity provides enough flexibility so that young children can work successfully. Effectively instructing children of varying ages requires a teacher to recognize and accept wide individual differences in skills, abilities and interests. Regardless of the level at which a child works, a teacher can use the child's interest in the activity to guide his or her thinking toward understanding a Bible truth.

Bible Learning Activities

THREE- and FOUR-YEAR-OLDS need free play and careful supervision. They often pursue different activities, having little interest in cooperative play. Provide books and puzzles for children who are not interested in the activities offered, but engage children in conversation related to the day's lesson as they work. KINDERGARTNERS enjoy experimenting with a variety of materials and tools. Their verbal skills and enjoyment of other children make play more purposeful and interactive.

THREES and FOURS use blocks in an exploratory manner, stacking and moving them in a seemingly random fashion. Occasionally extend children's play by offering specific building instructions as suggested in the lesson. KINDERGARTNERS usually plan what they will build and then use the construction to play out an imaginary event. They incorporate accessories such as toy cars and animals in the building.

THREES and FOURS are just beginning to use art supplies and often find the finished product of little interest. Encourage them to try new things, but don't expect beauty or design. KINDERGARTNERS enjoy exploring the use of art materials but may find the process tedious after a short while. To sustain their interest, offer encouragement and assistance as needed.

Large-Group Times

THREES and FOURS need a variety of brief activities during a large-group experience. Puppets provide visual interest, but keep puppet dialogue to a minimum. Because children do not have a backlog of experiences to help them recall an idea or object, show pictures and objects to illustrate conversation and activities.

KINDERGARTNERS enjoy talking about things they have seen and done and will enjoy interacting with puppets. When the conversation relates to a common experience, most children are interested in hearing other children recount events. Avoid letting any one child dominate the conversation.

Because repetition is essential to a child's learning process, he or she needs to hear and sing the same songs again and again. Repeat familiar songs for THREES and FOURS. Introduce more of the songs suggested in each lesson for KINDERGARTNERS.

Bible Story/Application

To accommodate the attention span of THREES and FOURS, keep the Bible story very brief. Illustrate story action with visuals from *Prekindergarten/Kindergarten Teaching Resources*. Ask simple questions to help children recall Bible facts that are obvious in the story and visuals.

Although KINDERGARTNERS have a slightly longer attention span, tell the Bible stories without elaboration. They enjoy the challenge of what-do-you-think questions.

Grades 1 and 2

Physical

The term "perpetual motion" may be used to describe children this age. Small-muscle coordination is still developing and improving. Girls are ahead of boys at this stage of development.

Teaching Tip: Give children opportunities for movement during every class session.

Social

Children are concerned with pleasing their leaders. Each child is also struggling to become socially acceptable to the peer group. The Golden Rule is a tough concept at this age. Being first and winning are very important. Taking turns is hard, but this skill improves by the end of the second grade. A child's social process moves gradually from *I* to *you* and *we*.

Teaching Tips: Provide opportunities for children to practice taking turns. Help each child accept the opinions and wishes of others and consider the welfare of the group as well as his or her own welfare. Call attention to times when the group cooperated successfully.

Spiritual

Children can sense the greatness, wonder and love of God when helped with visual and specific examples. The nonphysical nature of God is baffling, but God's presence in every area of life is generally accepted when parents and teachers communicate this belief by their attitudes and actions. Children can think of Jesus as a friend, but they need specific examples of how Jesus expresses love and care. This understanding leads many children to belief and acceptance of Jesus as personal Savior. Children can comprehend talking to God anywhere, anytime and in their own words; and they need regular opportunities to pray.

Teaching Tips: The gospel becomes real as children feel love from those who talk about God. Show your faith in a consistent, loving way to model the loving nature of God to children. Look for natural opportunities to talk with children about God's love for them and His desire for them to become members of His family.

Emotional

Children are experiencing new and frequently intense feelings as they grow in independence. Sometimes the child finds it hard to control his or her behavior. There is still a deep need for approval from adults and a growing need for approval by peers.

Teaching Tips: Seek opportunities to help each child in your group KNOW and FEEL you love him or her. Show genuine interest in each child and his or her activities and accomplishments. Learn children's names and use them frequently in positive ways.

Cognitive

There is an intense eagerness to learn, and children of this age ask lots of questions. They like to repeat stories and activities. The concept of time is limited. Thinking is here and now, rather than past or future. Listening and speaking skills are developing rapidly; girls are ahead of boys. Each child thinks everyone shares his or her view. Children see parts, rather than how the parts make up the whole, and they think very literally.

Teaching Tip: Talk simply and clearly, avoiding words the child may not understand.

Grades 3 and 4

Physical

Children at this level have good large- and small-muscle coordination. The girls are generally ahead of the boys. Children can work diligently for longer periods but can become impatient with delays or their own imperfect abilities.

Teaching Tip: When playing games that involve taking turns, keep teams small so that kids don't wait long to have a turn.

Social

Children's desire for status within the peer group becomes more intense. Most children remain shy with strangers and exhibit strong preferences for being with a few close friends. Some children still lack essential social skills needed to make and retain friendships.

Teaching Tip: Look for the child who needs a friend. Move near that child and include him or her in what you are doing.

Spiritual

Children are open to sensing the need for God's continuous help and guidance. They can recognize the need for a personal Savior. There may be a desire to become a member of God's family. Children who indicate an awareness of sin and a concern about accepting Jesus as Savior need careful guidance without pressure.

Teaching Tips: Give children opportunities to pray. Talk about the forgiving nature of God. Talk personally with a child who shows interest in trusting the Lord Jesus. Use the *God Loves You!* booklet to explain how to become a Christian.

Emotional

This is the age of teasing, nicknames, criticism and increased verbal skills to vent anger. By eight years of age, children have developed a sense of fair play and a value system of right and wrong. At nine years of age, children are searching for identity beyond membership in the family unit.

Teaching Tips: You have a great opportunity to be a Christian example at a time when children are eagerly searching for models! Encourage children's creativity and boost their self-concept. Let children know by your words and by your actions that "love is spoken here" and that you will not let others hurt them or let them hurt others.

Cognitive

Children are beginning to realize there may be valid opinions besides their own. They are becoming able to evaluate alternatives and are less likely than before to fasten onto one viewpoint as the only one possible. Children are also beginning to think in terms of "the whole." Children think more conceptually and have a high level of creativity. By this stage, however, many children have become self-conscious as their understanding has grown to exceed their abilities in some areas.

Teaching Tips: Encourage children to use their Bibles by finding and reading portions of Scripture. Help children understand the meaning of the verses they memorize.

Grades 5 and 6

Physical

Children have mastered most basic physical skills, are active and curious, and seek a variety of new experiences. Rapid growth can cause some 11-year-olds to tire easily.

Teaching Tip: Oftentimes in coed groups, boys tend to be less aggressive and girls tend to be friendlier. The mixture seems to bring out the best in both genders.

Social

Friendships and activities with their peers flourish. Children draw together and away from adults in the desire for independence. The child wants to be a part of a same-gender group and usually does not want to stand alone in competition.

Teaching Tip: When you play games that require score keeping, move on to the next round or activity without announcing the score or winner. If the activity is fun and compelling, most kids will never notice the omission.

Spiritual

Children can have deep feelings of love for God, can share the good news of Jesus with a friend and are capable of involvement in outreach and service projects. The child may seek guidance from God to make everyday and long-range decisions.

Teaching Tips: Provide opportunities for children to make choices and decisions based on Bible concepts. Involve children in work and service projects.

Emotional

Children are usually cooperative, easygoing, content, friendly and agreeable. Be aware that often 11-year-old children are experiencing unsteady emotions and can quickly shift from one mood to another.

Teaching Tips: Be patient with changes of feelings. Give many opportunities to make choices with only a few necessary limits. Take time to listen as students share their experiences and problems with you.

Cognitive

Children of this age are verbal! Making ethical decisions becomes a challenging task. They are able to express ideas and feelings in a creative way. By 11 years old, children have begun to be able to reason abstractly. They begin to think of themselves as grown-up and at the same time question adult concepts. Hero worship is strong.

Teaching Tips: Include lots of opportunities for talking, questioning and discussing in a safe, accepting environment. Ask children for their ideas of how things could be done better.

SonForce Kids Craft Leader's Guide

If you'll be leading crafts at SonForce Kids Vacation Bible School, *Special Agent Crafts for Kids* contains more than enough crafts for each age level. For additional hints about leading a group of children in craft projects, see "Be Prepared" on page 5.

The projects in this book can be done in individual classrooms or in a Craft Center. Here's how a Craft Center works:

- Select projects that will appeal to several age levels. (Sometimes you'll find one project that all children will enjoy making. Other times you'll need to select one project for the younger children and one for the older children.)
- Recruit adults and/or youths to prepare for and run the Craft Center.
- Decorate your center with samples of crafts your kids will be making.
- As classes visit the Craft Center, lead them in making projects, tailoring instructions and conversation to the children's age level.

The Craft Coordinator—A Very Important Person

As Craft Coordinator, you play a key role in determining the quality of your craft program. Here are four crucial steps in achieving success at your task:

1. Plan ahead. Familiarize yourself with each day's craft project and plan any necessary changes.
2. Be well-organized (see the "SonForce Kids Countdown Schedule").
3. Secure your supplies in advance. Prepare a bulletin notice listing items you need donated from members of your congregation. Also, people are often happy to help if you personally ask them to donate or purchase specific items.
4. Communicate with everyone involved. People who do not know what to do may not ask for help.

SonForce Kids Countdown Schedule

16 weeks before:

1. List all staff needs. (Determine if crafts will be led by regular teachers or by special craft leaders and if students from the Youth Department will serve as craft helpers.)
2. Meet with the VBS Director to compile a list of prospective staff.
3. Begin personal contacts to recruit needed staff.

12 weeks before:

1. Select projects from this book and list needed supplies.
2. Determine which items are already on hand and which need to be secured.

8 weeks before:

1. Distribute a bulletin notice listing needed supplies.
2. Begin organizing supplies as they are acquired. Separate inventories for each age group are often helpful, especially in large programs.

6 weeks before:

1. Review staffing needs with the VBS Director and plan involvement in training session.
2. Assign leaders to make a sample of each craft project that they will teach to children.
3. Distribute second notice regarding supplies.

4 weeks before:

1. Participate in training session, showing samples of at least the first-day craft projects.
2. Distribute third notice regarding supplies.
3. Make any needed personal contacts to gather required supplies.

2 weeks before:

1. Purchase any supplies still needed. Adjust supplies as needed.

During VBS:

1. Make sure needed supplies are available for staff.
2. Secure additional supplies as needed.

Course Description

Invite your students to join SonForce Kids—God's courageous team of disciples standing side-by-side to serve Him. As SonForce special agents, they will follow in the words of Joshua 1:9: *Be strong and courageous. Do not be terrified; do not be discouraged, for the Lord your God will be with you wherever you go.*

The SonForce Kids headquarters is located on a satellite orbiting high above the earth. In this hi-tech command center, SonForce agents gather to prepare for their five Daily Missions: Trust! Unite! Train! Follow! Lead! Throughout VBS, your students will have the opportunity to grow in their understanding of what it means to serve God with courage as they advance from Level 1 to Level 5 agents.

From the courage shown by baby Moses' family, Level 1 agents will learn to **TRUST in God's Plans**. Following Esther's example, Level 2 agents will be encouraged to **UNITE with God's People**. To help them make wise choices like Daniel did, Level 3 agents will learn to **TRAIN for God's Service**. Just as Jeremiah obeyed God even when it was difficult, Level 4 agents will learn to **FOLLOW in God's Path**. Finally, like Joshua and Caleb, Level 5 agents will get ready to **LEAD Others to God's Promises**.

So get ready for an out-of-this-world adventure. SonForce Kids—courageous kids on a mission for God!

Decorating Your Craft Center—Tech Lab

Turn your Craft Center into the Tech Lab, where young scientists create the many unusual gadgets used by SonForce agents. Enlarge the Invention Diagram Patterns found in *Reproducible Resources* onto butcher paper, and attach them to the walls.

On tables and shelves, set out plenty of tinkering items such as small tools, springs, gears, bolts, hoses and wires. Include some science equipment such as a telescope, microscope and beakers. Add a few ordinary objects that can be transformed into SonForce gadgets, such as radios, shoes, sunglasses and cell phones.

Set up a display with a few science toys and novelties such as Hoberman spheres, dippy birds, plasma lamps, lava lamps and gyroscopes. Complete the room with rope lights or Christmas lights. (Optional: Follow the directions found in *Reproducible Resources* to add one or more robots to your Tech Lab.)

Course Overview and Suggested Crafts

Below is an overview of SonForce Kids VBS with suggested projects for each age level. Each craft has been selected to reinforce the Bible story, lesson focus or memory verse of the day. All projects are fully described in this book.

SECTION	BIBLE STORY	FOCUS	BIBLE MEMORY VERSE	SUGGESTED CRAFTS
1 TRUST In God's Plans	Moses: Boy in a Basket Exodus 1—2:10	We can have courage in all situations by trusting in God's love and plans for us.	**Early Childhood** Trust in the Lord. (See Jeremiah 17:7.) **Elementary** "Blessed is the man who trusts in the Lord, whose confidence is in him." Jeremiah 17:7	**Early Childhood** Baby Moses in a Basket **Primary** SonForce Agent Badge **Middler** Moses Marble Maze **Preteen** Mission Patches
2 UNITE With God's People	Esther: Queen at Risk Esther 2—8	We can have courage to stand up for others by uniting with God's people.	**Early Childhood** With love, help each other. Galatians 5:13 **Elementary** "Be devoted to one another in brotherly love. Honor one another above yourselves." Romans 12:10	**Early Childhood** Jeweled Wristband **Primary** Palace Ornament **Middler** Courage Magnets **Preteen** Eye-See Can
3 TRAIN For God's Service	Daniel: Servant of God Daniel 1	We can have courage to make wise choices by training to serve God.	**Early Childhood** Listen to advice and you will be wise. (See Proverbs 19:20.) **Elementary** "Listen to advice and accept instruction, and in the end you will be wise." Proverbs 19:20	**Early Childhood** Veggie Concentration **Primary** Blast-Off Rocket **Middler** Create-a-Bot **Preteen** Wise Words Bookmark
4 FOLLOW In God's Path	Jeremiah: Prophet in Trouble Jeremiah 36—39	We can have courage to follow in God's path, even when it is difficult.	**Early Childhood** Obey me, and I will be your God. Jeremiah 7:23 **Elementary** "Obey me, and I will be your God and you will be my people. Walk in all the ways I command you, that it may go well with you." Jeremiah 7:23	**Early Childhood** Jeremiah's Scroll **Primary** Robo-Dog **Middler** Jeremiah's Message **Preteen** Spacewalk T-Shirt
5 LEAD Others to God's Promises	Joshua: Spy in a Strange Land Numbers 13—14:9	We can have courage to lead others to God's promises.	**Early Childhood** Be strong and courageous . . . for the Lord your God will be with you wherever you go. Joshua 1:9 **Elementary** "Be strong and courageous. Do not be terrified; do not be discouraged, for the Lord your God will be with you wherever you go." Joshua 1:9	**Early Childhood** Joshua and Caleb Take a Peek **Primary** SFA Promise Viewer **Middler** Pocket Computer **Preteen** Time Zone Gadget

Moses: Boy in a Basket

Scripture

Exodus 1—2:10

Bible Memory Verse

Blessed is the man who trusts in the Lord, whose confidence is in him. Jeremiah 17:7

Lesson Focus

We can have courage in all situations by trusting in God's love and plans for us.

Bible Aims

During this session, each student may

1. DESCRIBE the way baby Moses' mother and sister showed courage to protect him;
2. LIST and DISCUSS situations in which kids can have courage by trusting in God's love and plans for them;
3. THANK God for His love, and ask God to help him or her have courage in all situations;
4. PRAY to become a member of God's family, as the Holy Spirit leads.

Bible Story Recap

The Egyptian Pharaoh decided that the Israelites had grown too big in numbers and threatened his power, so he made them slaves. Despite merciless work, their numbers increased. So Pharaoh decreed that all Israelite baby boys should be thrown into the Nile River!

One Israelite family protected their baby boy for three months. Then the mother put her trust in God. She wove a basket, waterproofed it and laid the baby inside. Placing the basket in the river, she instructed the baby's sister, Miriam, to watch over him. Soon Pharaoh's daughter, the princess, discovered the infant. Miriam offered to find an Israelite woman to care for the baby, and she brought back the infant's own mother. The princess named the baby Moses, and he grew up to become the leader of God's people.

Teacher Devotional

Every parent knows how stressful it can be to adjust to a new baby, but the experience of Moses' family far exceeds anything most of us will ever know. The family had a beautiful new baby boy, but Pharaoh had ordered that all Hebrew baby boys be thrown into the Nile River. Imagine trying to quiet a tiny crying baby quickly enough so that soldiers wouldn't come to kill him! As Moses grew, his parents' choices were few; if he were discovered, he would die. They did have an idea, however: They put him in the Nile in a waterproof basket. They did all they could, TRUSTING God to do something miraculous.

God had big plans for Moses. He protected Moses and used him mightily. Now think about your own life. You've seen God protect you, perhaps even through some times as dangerous as those Moses faced. Pause to consider what His plans may be for you! Those plans may not look big to you—they may even be hidden from your sight right now—but rest assured, they are of eternal importance!

There are no little plans in God's eyes. What you are doing at this moment is part of the amazing tapestry He is weaving for you and through you. In His plan, your words and actions will affect many others. He has led you and protected you just as He protected Moses. Trust in God as you watch His plans unfold!

Esther: Queen at Risk

Scripture

Esther 2—8

Bible Memory Verse

Be devoted to one another in brotherly love. Honor one another above yourselves. Romans 12:10

Lesson Focus

We can have courage to stand up for others by uniting with God's people.

Bible Aims

During this session, each student may

1. TELL that God's people helped Esther have courage to stand up for them;
2. IDENTIFY ways that kids can stand up for others;
3. ASK God to help him or her have courage to stand up for others;
4. PRAY to become a member of God's family, as the Holy Spirit leads.

Bible Story Recap

From many beautiful young women, Esther was chosen as the new wife of Xerxes, king of Persia. Esther's cousin Mordecai worked for the king. When a decree was made that everyone would bow to the king's highest official, Haman, Mordecai refused. As a Jew, he believed he should bow only to God. Haman was so angry at Mordecai that he tricked the king into signing a death sentence for Mordecai and all the Jewish people!

Esther called for the Jewish people to unite for three days of fasting and prayer. Esther went to speak to the king, even though she could be killed! After the king spared her life, Esther invited him and Haman to two banquets. At the second, Esther revealed Haman's plan. The king ordered Haman's execution, and the Jewish people were saved!

Teacher Devotional

During the rule of Xerxes (also known by the Hebrew name Ahasuerus) of Persia occurs the beautiful and charming story of Esther. Although God's name is not mentioned in the book of Esther, His presence can be found behind each word. God has a part in all the events of human life.

Esther stands out as God's chosen one. The beauty of Esther was that she wasn't spoiled by her great position. Although she became queen of a great king, she didn't forget the kindness of her cousin Mordecai, who had brought her up from childhood. Esther was faced with the opportunity to help rescue the lives of her oppressed people, the Jews, but only at great risk to her own life. Accepting this dangerous task, she carried it out with courage and wisdom. Even as she went forward on behalf of the Jews, she asked them to pray and fast on HER behalf. Esther knew that God was listening to the prayers of His people and that with His help they could UNITE and defeat their enemy.

It was a daring act for her to enter unsummoned into the presence of the king. Yet she knew she must choose the right course, despite the danger to herself. She knew this was a time to have courage and stand up for others. Esther was prepared and was brought to the kingdom for just such an hour.

We would all do well to pause and ask, "Why has God allowed me to live at this particular hour?" When faced with challenges that require the courage to do what is right, it is always easier when we are supported by the prayers of fellow believers.

Daniel: Servant of God

Scripture

Daniel 1

Bible Memory Verse

Listen to advice and accept instruction, and in the end you will be wise. Proverbs 19:20

Lesson Focus

We can have courage to make wise choices by training to serve God.

Bible Aims

During this session, each student may

1. SUMMARIZE the wise choices Daniel courageously made because he had trained to serve God;
2. IDENTIFY ways that kids can train for God's service;
3. PLAN a way to train for God's service, and ask God to help him or her have courage to make wise choices;
4. PRAY to become a member of God's family, as the Holy Spirit leads.

Bible Story Recap

Daniel, Shadrach, Meshach and Abednego were taken from their homes in Jerusalem to Babylon. Although captives, their situation improved when they were chosen to go into training to serve the Babylonian king.

When the king declared that all the young men chosen to serve him must eat food from his table, Daniel and his friends had a problem. Eating this food, which had been offered to false gods, would have been disobedient to God. So Daniel struck a deal with the guard who brought them their food. For 10 days, the young men ate only vegetables and drank only water. When the 10 days were over, Daniel and his friends were stronger and healthier looking than all the others. They were given permission to continue showing their obedience to God.

Teacher Devotional

Imagine living through an enemy attack that destroys your home and makes you a prisoner of war. Daniel and his friends lived through just this horror, probably while they were still teenagers. The best and brightest of Jerusalem's royal court, they saw their promising futures and privileged circumstances evaporate as they left Jerusalem behind.

Captive in a strange land, they were without a country or a chosen future. The Babylonians were clearly working to eliminate their Israelite identities and make them ready to serve Nebuchadnezzar. The boys probably had no choice about being dressed in Babylonian fashion or given Babylonian names. But there was one way they could hold on to who they really were: They could honor the dietary laws of Israel. It may seem like a small thing to us, but it was one way to be obedient and remain true to the training they had received to serve God.

God often brings such small acts to our attention, acts we can do to continue to put into practice our love and obedience to God. These small acts may not seem any more significant than the food choices of Daniel and his friends. It's usually easier to ignore such small things and go along with "the program." But remembering the ways in which we have been trained will help us obey God with the courage of Daniel. When we're tempted to go along with the crowd, God gives us courage and strength to stand up for His ways like Daniel and his friends did.

Jeremiah: Prophet in Trouble

Scripture

Jeremiah 36—39

Bible Memory Verse

Obey me, and I will be your God and you will be my people. Walk in all the ways I command you, that it may go well with you. Jeremiah 7:23

Lesson Focus

We can have courage to follow in God's path, even when it is difficult.

Bible Aims

During this session, each student may

1. DISCOVER that Jeremiah obeyed God's commands, even when it was difficult;
2. DISCUSS situations in which kids might find it hard to obey God's commands;
3. ASK God to help him or her have courage to obey God;
4. PRAY to become a member of God's family, as the Holy Spirit leads.

Bible Story Recap

Jeremiah was a prophet of God who had many times told people to follow in His path. When God told Jeremiah that He had a warning for the people of Judah, Jeremiah obeyed. His helper, Baruch, wrote on a scroll the words that God gave Jeremiah.

When the scroll was finished, Baruch read it aloud at the Temple, and then later the king heard God's warnings. But as sections of the scroll were read, the king took a knife, cut out each section and burned it! So God told Jeremiah to make a new scroll, which he and Baruch did. Jeremiah obeyed and followed God, even when it was difficult. But the people didn't pay attention to God, and the warnings came true.

Teacher Devotional

Jeremiah was called from the obscurity of his native town to assume, at a critical hour in the nation's life, the overwhelming responsibilities of a prophet. His father, Hilkiah, was a priest, so Jeremiah inherited the traditions of an illustrious ancestry. His early life was likely also influenced by strong religious leaders. But God had something even better for Jeremiah than to spend his life as a priest serving at the altar. God appointed this young man to be a prophet of the Lord in this trying hour in the history of the Chosen People.

Frequently, the Israelites chose to disobey God, even though God's commands had been designed for their well-being. When they stopped following God, they ended up in great trouble. So God warned them through Jeremiah's messages. Just as the people of Israel had to choose whether or not they would listen to the warning in Jeremiah's messages, people today face the choice between following God's ways or pursuing their own ways.

The God of Jeremiah is always ready to give each one of us, and the children we teach, the courage we need to follow in His path, even in difficult circumstances. God's promise of courage springs from His love. He is ready to forgive us when we make a wrong choice, and even better, He is fully able to help us follow Him wholeheartedly so that we can live in the best way possible!

Joshua: Spy in a Strange Land

Scripture

Numbers 13—14:9

Bible Memory Verse

Be strong and courageous. Do not be terrified; do not be discouraged, for the Lord your God will be with you wherever you go. Joshua 1:9

Lesson Focus

We can have courage to lead others to God's promises.

Bible Aims

During this session, each student may

1. DISCOVER that Joshua and Caleb had courage to believe in God's promises and to tell others about them;
2. IDENTIFY situations in which kids can help others believe in God's promises;
3. THANK God for His promises, and ask God for courage to help others believe in His promises;
4. PRAY to become a member of God's family, as the Holy Spirit leads.

Bible Story Recap

Having escaped slavery in Egypt, Moses and the Israelites were ready to enter the Promised Land. Moses chose 12 leaders to go into the land and observe the area and its people.

When the men returned, they told of the fruitful and beautiful land. But 10 of them thought that the people were too powerful and the cities too strong to conquer. However, Joshua and Caleb believed in God's promises, and they tried to lead the others to believe in God's promises, too. The Israelites grumbled that they'd rather be in Egypt than be defeated by the people in the land! At Moses' request, God forgave the people for their unbelief. But 40 years would pass before He gave them the land, and only Joshua and Caleb would lead the Israelites into the Promised Land.

Teacher Devotional

The book of Joshua provides a wealth of encouragement and wisdom for the followers of God. Yet this book is not only about following God but also about leading others to Him. As we follow the story of Joshua, we see a man who is determined to trust God's promises and equally determined to lead His people to receive those promises.

Picture this scene: The children of Israel have recently been freed from slavery in Egypt and are on the verge of inheriting the Promised Land. But, because of their fear, the poor Israelites are ready to turn back to the slavery they have just left behind. They cannot invade this land filled with "giants" and take the walled cities. The conquest of the land seems impossible!

Now, Caleb and Joshua had seen the same "giants" and had inspected the same fortifications, yet they insisted that the land could be taken! Because of their courage and trust in God's promises, they were ready to LEAD these people.

God sometimes calls us to lead others in fearful situations, too. When He does, we have the same words that were given to Joshua in answer to his prayer for help in his great undertaking: *Be strong and courageous. Do not be terrified; do not be discouraged, for the Lord your God will be with you wherever you go* (Joshua 1:9). These words are just as true for us!

SECTION ONE

Prekindergarten/Kindergarten

Crafts for Young Children

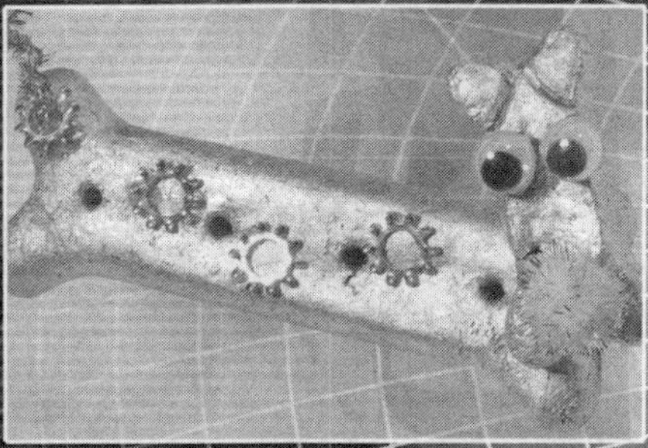

Craft projects for young children are a blend of "I wanna do it myself!" and "I need help!" Crafts usually require a certain amount of adult assistance—preparing a pattern, doing some cutting, preselecting magazine pictures, tying a knot, etc. But always take care to avoid robbing the child of the satisfaction of his or her own unique efforts. Do only what is absolutely necessary! The adult's desire to have a nice finished project should not override the child's pleasure in experimenting with color and texture. Avoid the temptation to do the project for the child or to improve on his or her efforts.

Some of these crafts have enrichment and simplification ideas. An enrichment idea provides a way to make the craft more challenging for the older child. A simplification idea helps the younger child complete the craft successfully.

Although most projects in this book allow plenty of leeway for children to be creative, some children may become frustrated with the limitations of a structured craft. This frustration may be a signal that the child needs an opportunity to work with more basic, less structured materials: blank paper and markers, play dough, or precut magazine pictures to make into a collage. In any task a young child undertakes, remember that the process the child goes through is more important than the finished product.

Hidden Picture Viewer (10-15 MINUTES)

Materials

- Kindness Picture (p. 19)
- red cellophane

For every 2 children—

- four lightweight paper plates
- red ink pad
- stamps with simple lines (not solid shapes)

Standard Supplies

- scissors
- ruler
- craft knife
- transparent tape
- glue

Preparation

Photocopy one Kindness Picture for each child. Cut cellophane into one 4x6-inch (10x15-cm) rectangle for each child. Use scissors or craft knife to cut a 3x5-inch (7.5x12.5-cm) window in the center of two paper plates for each child (sketch a).

Conversation

Carlos, you are waiting patiently for a turn to use the stamps! When we are patient with others we are doing what is right. What are some ways you can do what is right at home? (Clean my room without complaining. Help my brother pick up leaves in the yard.) **You can ask God for help to do what is right. I'm glad God loves us and will always help us.**

Instruct each child in the following procedures:

- Stamp all over top of Kindness Picture (sketch b). Let ink dry.
- Tape a piece of cellophane over the window cut in one plate (sketch c).
- Glue a second plate on top of first, so that windows in plates line up (sketch d).
- Lay viewer over picture. Move viewer around to see hidden picture.

Enrichment Idea

Children use black pens to draw their own pictures on paper and repeat process.

a.

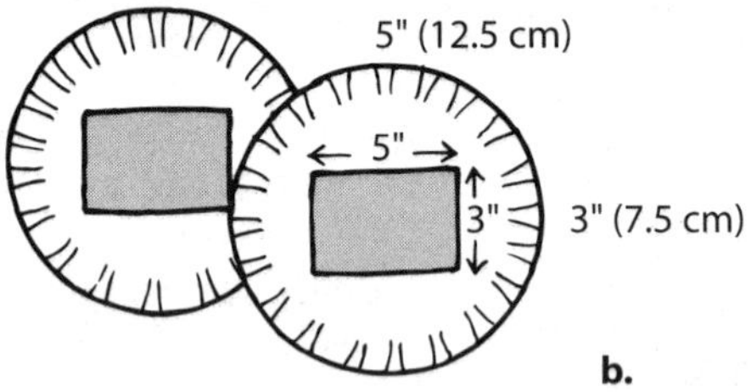

b.

c.

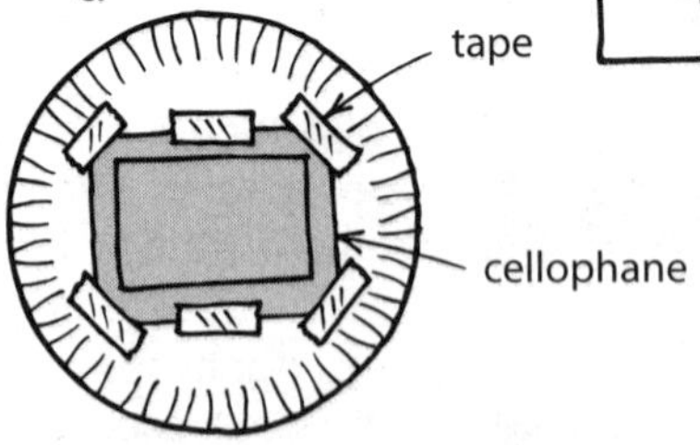

d.

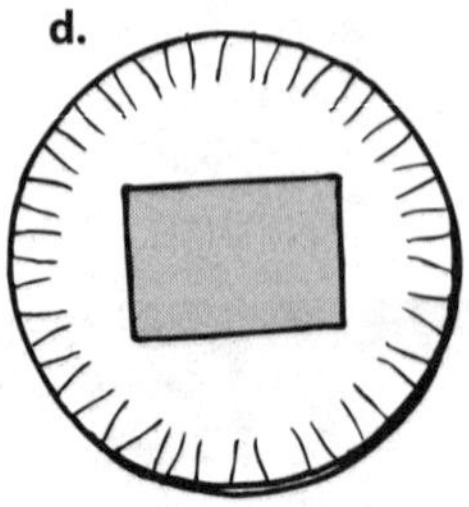

glue plates together

Kindness Picture

Band-Aid Bot (10-15 MINUTES)

Materials

- Front Bot Pattern (p. 21)
- Back Bot Pattern (p. 21)
- craft foam in various colors
- metallic curling ribbon or cord
- fine-tip permanent markers
- large sequins

For each child—

- metallic chenille wire
- 1-inch (2.5-cm) self-adhesive round craft magnet
- four to six adhesive bandages

Standard Supplies

- scissors
- hole punch
- measuring stick
- transparent tape
- glue

Preparation

Trace onto craft foam one Front and Back Bot Pattern for each child and cut out. Mark dots on foam as indicated on patterns and punch holes at the dots. Save punched circles. Cut metallic ribbon or cord into one 2-foot (.6-m) length for each child. Wrap one end of each cord or ribbon with transparent tape to make a needle for easier lacing. (Note: Before children begin to lace Band-Aid Bots together, demonstrate the lacing technique a few times.)

Conversation

Bryan, listening to my instructions helped you make your Band-Aid Bot. Our Bible says, *Listen to advice and you will be wise* (see Proverbs 19:20). **When you listen, you are being wise. Being wise means you do what God says is good and right. Thank you for being such a good listener!**

Instruct each child in the following procedures:

- Choose one Back and Front Bot Pattern. Line up Bot Patterns using punched holes as a guide.
- With teacher's help, insert ends of chenille wire through top holes on each side of foam pieces (sketch a).
- With teacher's help, thread ribbon or cord through hole below chenille wire on one side of foam shape. With teacher's help, knot end as shown in sketch b.
- Use ribbon or cord to lace edges together (sketch c).
- With teacher's help, tie a knot in cord to secure and trim off excess.
- Glue two foam circles to top of Back Pattern to make robot eyes (sketch d). Let dry. Use marker to draw a dot on each eye.
- Glue large sequins onto robot for decoration.
- Bend ends of chenille wires as desired to make hands for robot.
- Peel and stick magnetic circle on the back of robot.
- Slide adhesive bandages into pocket below robot's eyes.
- Put Band-Aid Bot on refrigerator so that bandages will be ready when needed.

Simplification Idea

For younger children, punch only six holes in Band-Aid Bots.

Enrichment Ideas

Children punch some or all of holes. They glue additional foam dots to the body of robot for decoration. Children wind chenille-wire arms around a pen to shape into springs.

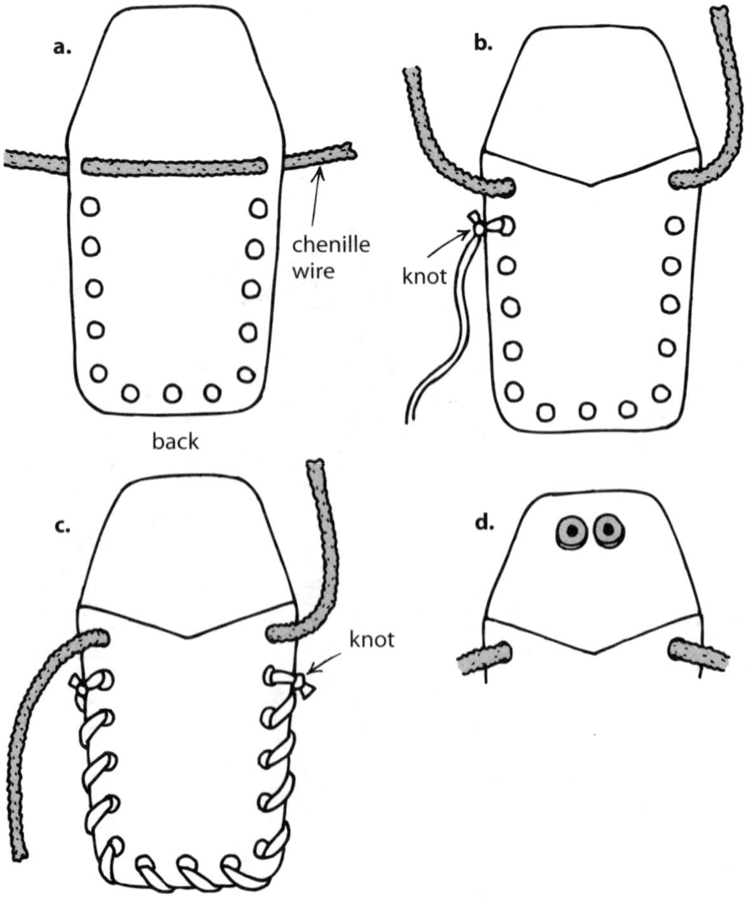

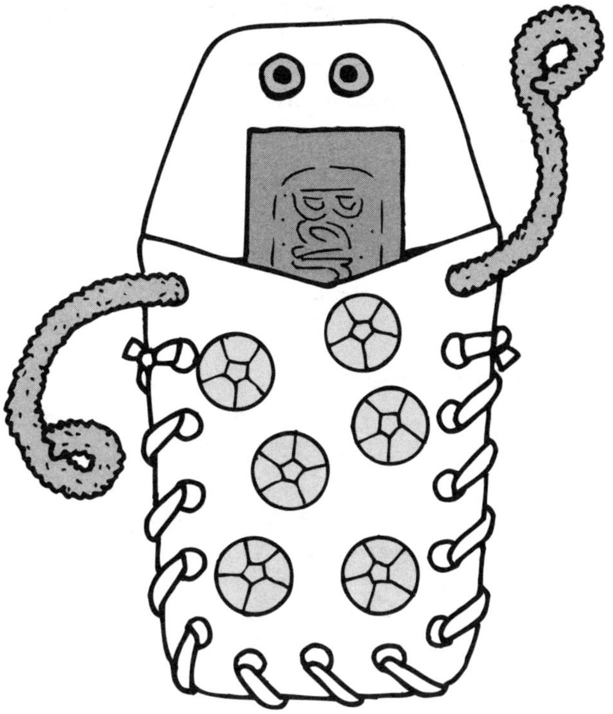

Front Bot Pattern

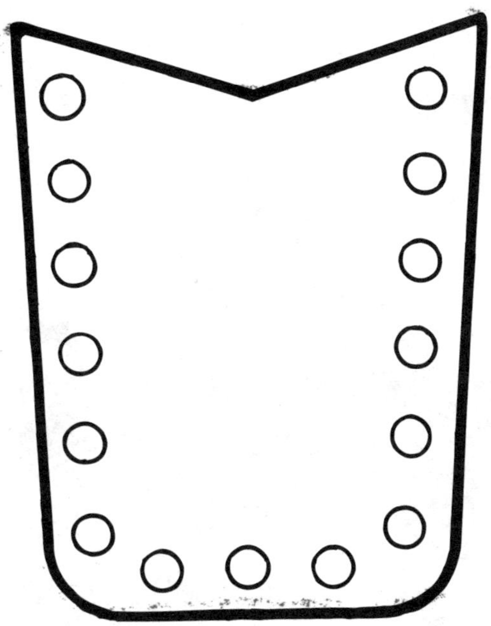

Back Bot Pattern

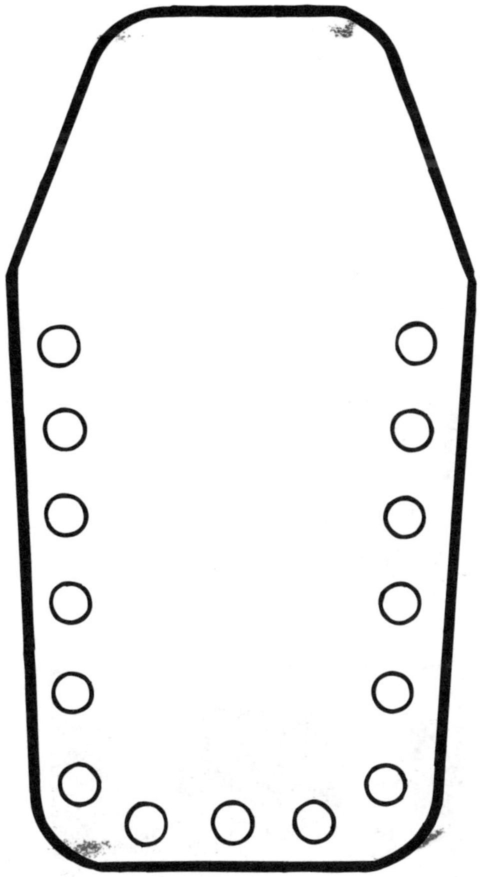

SonForce Puppet Theater (10-15 MINUTES)

Materials

- Stage Pattern (p. 23)
- Puppet Patterns (p. 22)
- space stickers (stars, planets, rockets)

For each child—

- two 3-ounce (90-ml) disposable cups (plastic or unwaxed paper)

Standard Supplies

- white card stock
- scissors
- markers
- tape

Preparation

Photocopy onto card stock one Stage Pattern and one set of Puppet Patterns for each child. Cut out Puppet Patterns.

Conversation

Zachary, thank you for taking turns with the crayons. Taking turns is a way to obey God. What is another way you can obey God? Our Bible says, *Obey me, and I will be your God* (Jeremiah 7:23)**. When you obey God, you are doing what God's Word says.**

a.

b.

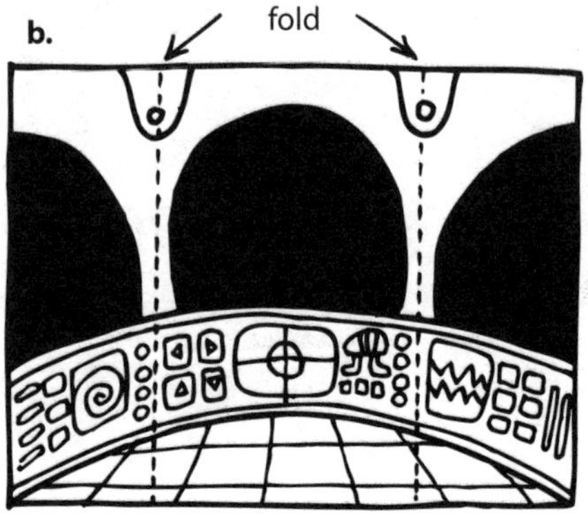

Instruct each child in the following procedures:

- Color Stage Pattern and decorate windows with space stickers.
- Color Puppet Patterns.
- Tape puppets to sides of overturned cups (sketch a).
- With teacher's help, fold Stage Pattern so that it will stand (sketch b). Play with puppets in front of backgrounds.

Enrichment Idea

Instead of space stickers, children use glitter pens to draw stars onto windows of Stage Pattern.

Puppet Patterns

Stage Pattern

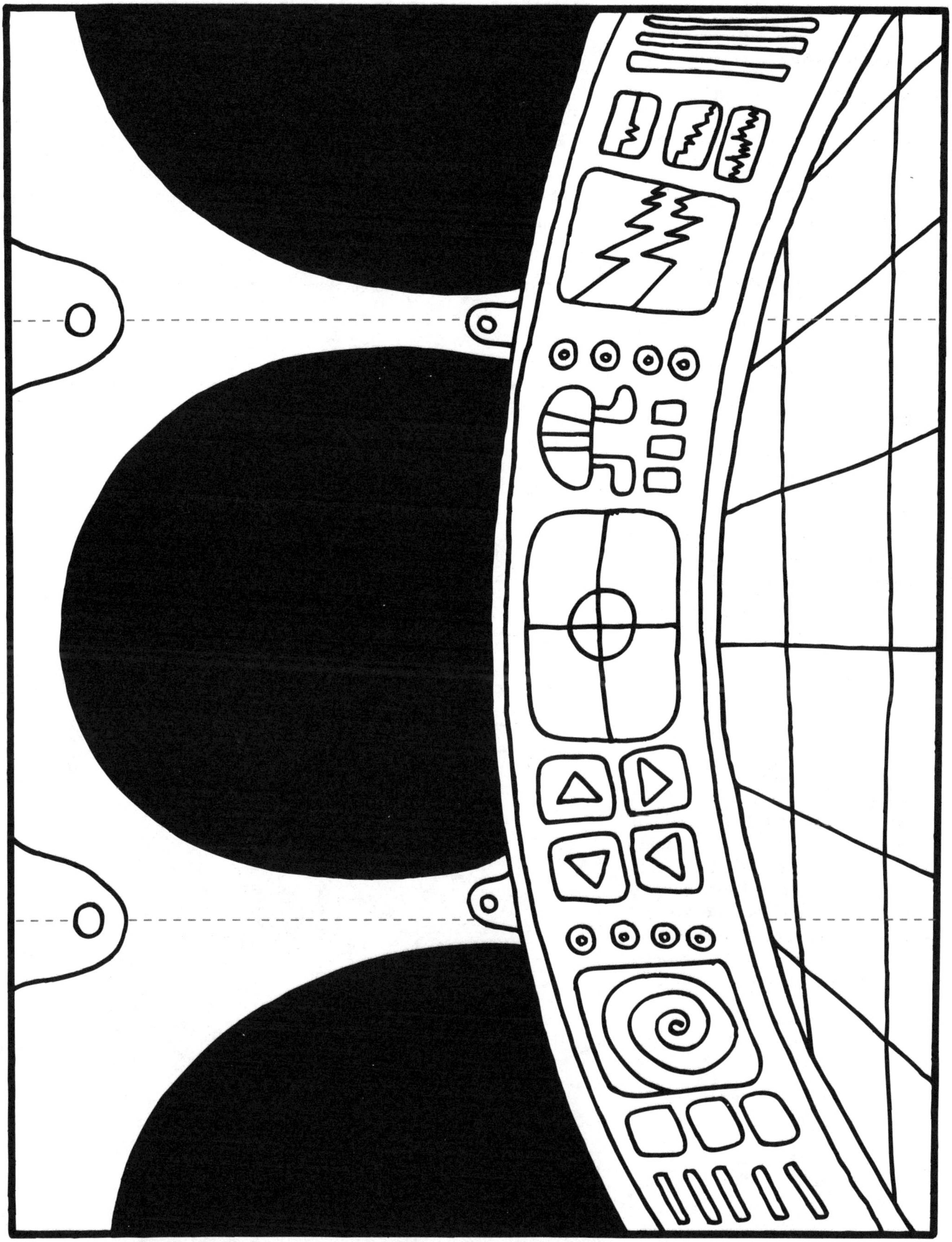

Jeweled Wristband (10–15 MINUTES)

Materials

- craft foam in various bright colors
- rickrack and braided trim in various bright colors
- metallic elastic cord
- self-adhesive jewels

Standard Supplies

- scissors
- ruler
- shallow containers
- hole punch
- craft glue

Preparation

Cut craft foam into one 1½x5-inch (4x12.5-cm) strip for each child. Cut rickrack and braided trim into several 2-inch (5-cm) lengths for each child. Cut elastic cord into one 6-inch (15-cm) length for each child. Place jewels, rickrack and trim into shallow containers.

Conversation

Queen Esther wore beautiful jewels when she went to see the king. Jennifer, thank you for giving your red jewel to Ashley. You helped Ashley finish her wristband. When you help your friends, you are showing God's love. Our Bible says, *With love, help each other* (Galatians 5:13)**.**

Instruct each child in the following procedures:

- With teacher's help, punch holes at each end of wristband (sketch a).
- Glue jewels, rickrack and braided trim onto wristbands (sketch b). Trim any uneven edges.
- With teacher's help, thread elastic cord through punched holes and tie closed (sketch c).

Enrichment Idea

Children make a second wristband to give to a friend.

a.

b.

c.

Carrier Tube (10–15 MINUTES)

Materials

- one or more decorative papers (metallic or foil wrapping paper, neon copier paper, etc.)
- metallic curling ribbon
- foil star stickers

For each child—

- potato-chip can with lid

Standard Supplies

- scissors
- measuring stick
- glue sticks
- transparent tape
- hole punch

Preparation

Cut wrapping paper into one 8¾x10-inch (22x25.5-cm) rectangle for each child. Cut ribbon into one 3-foot (.9-m) length for each child. Use scissors to cut holes in sides of can as shown in sketch a.

Conversation

What will you carry in your tube, James? You can take your tube with you wherever you go. Our Bible tells us a promise that God will be with us wherever we go. Where are some places you like to go? God loves us. We can believe His promises.

Instruct each child in the following procedures:

- Decorate wrapping-paper rectangle with star stickers.
- With teacher's help, glue wrapping-paper rectangle around outside of potato-chip can, aligning edges. Tape seam to secure (sketch b).
- Thread ends of metallic ribbon through holes, pull ends to top and tie knots to secure (sketch c).
- Put items in your Carrier Tube and slip over your shoulder to carry.

Enrichment Idea

Provide markers and paper for children to draw pictures or write messages to put in carrier tubes.

Budget Tip

Instead of metallic or foil wrapping paper, use aluminum foil to cover tubes.

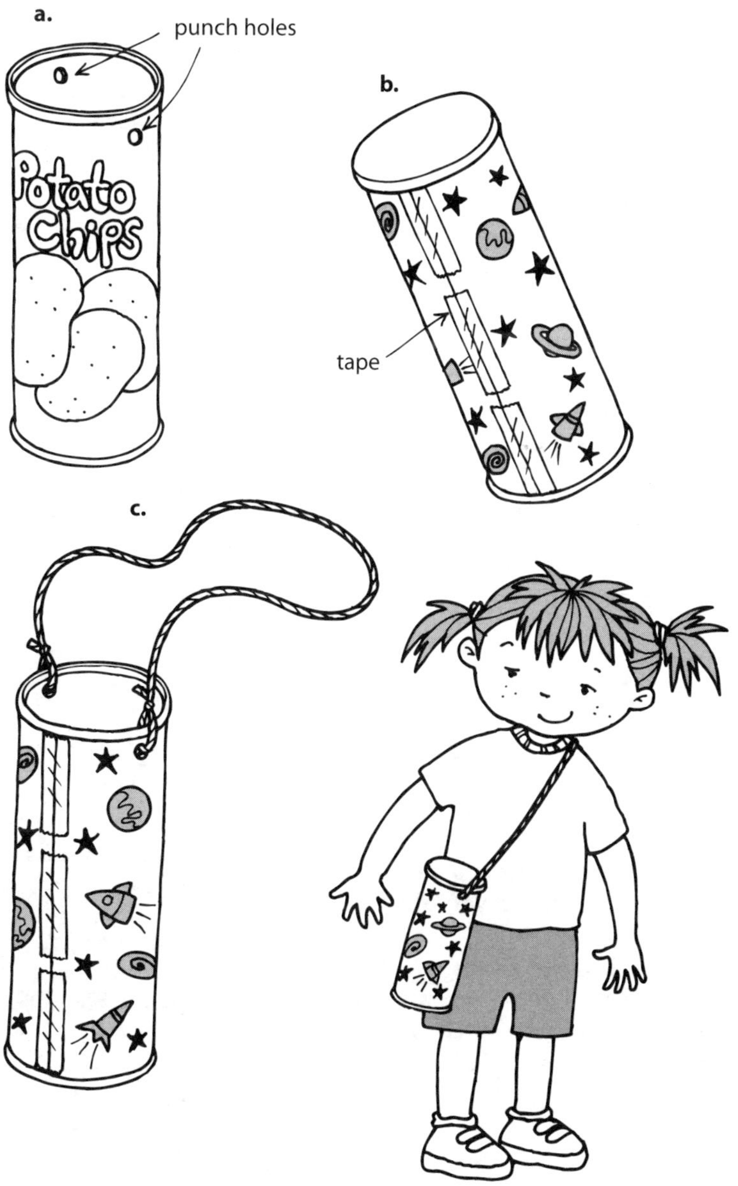

Disguise Kit (15-20 MINUTES)

Materials

- Disguise Patterns (p. 27)
- white card stock
- elastic cord
- peel-and-stick geometric foam stickers (available from school-supply stores)

For each child—

- plain paper gift bag or white lunch bag
- bandana

Standard Supplies

- scissors
- measuring stick
- markers or crayons
- hole punch
- glue sticks

Preparation

Photocopy one set of Disguise Patterns onto card stock for each child and cut out. Cut elastic cord into two 18-inch (45.5-cm) lengths for each child.

Instruct each child in the following procedures:

- Use markers or crayons to color mustaches.
- Punch two holes in each mustache at the dots.
- Thread elastic cord through the holes in mustaches (sketch a). With teacher's help, knot ends of cords together so that they fit comfortably around your head and under your nose.
- Use markers or crayons to color glasses. With teacher's help, glue earpieces to sides of glasses (sketch b).
- Use markers or crayons and stickers to color and decorate bags.
- Place your finished mustaches, glasses and bandana into the bag for easy carrying and to keep hidden when not in use. (Note: The bandana can be worn in a variety of ways, for example, on the head or around the neck.)

Enrichment Ideas

Children use glitter pens to color glasses. Before class, cut colored cellophane to fit eyeholes of glasses. To make sunglasses, children glue cellophane over eyeholes.

Budget Tip

Instead of bandana, use a 2-foot (.6-m) square of lightweight fabric for children to include in Disguise Kit.

a.

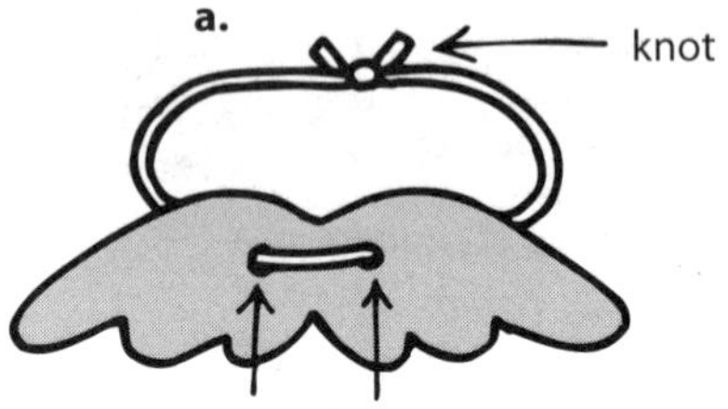

b.

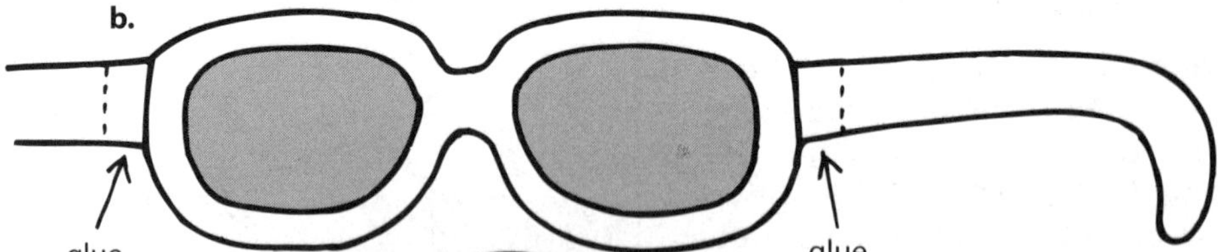

Conversation

Jesse, where will you wear your disguises? Even when you wear a disguise, God knows you and He is with you. Our Bible says that God is with us wherever we go! That means when we are at school, at home, at church or anywhere, God is there, too!

Disguise Patterns

Baby Moses in a Basket (15–20 MINUTES)

Materials

- Basket Pattern (p. 29)
- yellow card stock
- felt in various colors, including peach
- fiberfill stuffing
- black fine-tip permanent marker

For each child—

- white baby sock
- small rubber band

Standard Supplies

- scissors
- ruler
- glue
- transparent tape

Preparation

Photocopy one Basket Pattern onto yellow card stock for each child. Cut and fold baskets (sketch a). Cut peach felt into one 1½-inch (4-cm) circle for each child. Cut additional colors of felt into one 5-inch (12.5-cm) square for each child.

Conversation

God showed that He loved baby Moses. God helped keep baby Moses safe. God loves us, too. Brianna, when are some times you can remember God loves you? (When I go to school. When I'm afraid. When I go to the doctor.) **We can always trust in God's love and care for us.**

Instruct each child in the following procedures:

- Fill baby sock almost to the top with stuffing.
- Use marker to draw a face on peach circle (sketch b).
- With teacher's help, wrap rubber band around top of sock (sketch c).
- Glue face on sock directly below rubber band (sketch d).
- Fold top of sock down to make a cap (sketch e).
- Fold and tape ends of basket as shown in sketch f.
- Wrap Baby Moses in a felt square and place him inside basket.

Enrichment Idea

Children glue bits of straw around inside and outside card stock for a "woven" basket.

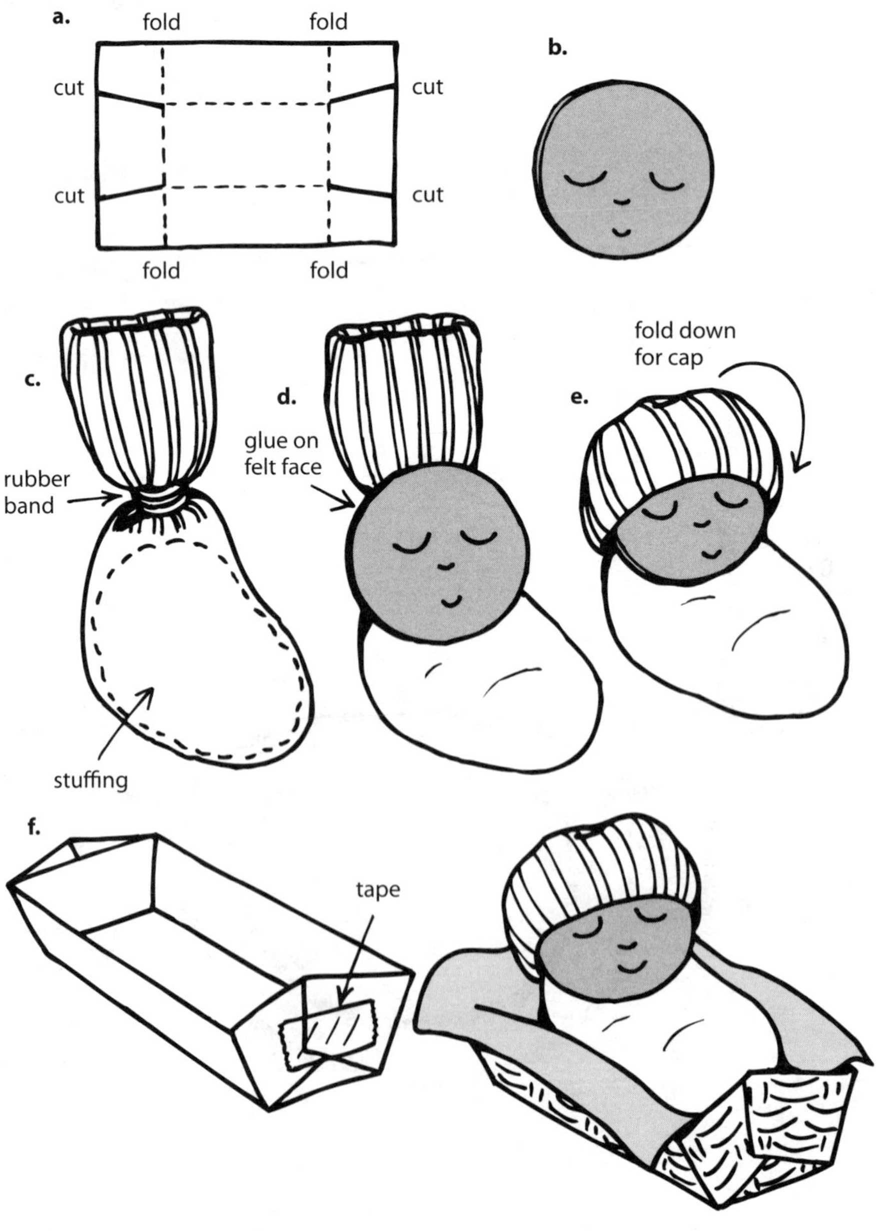

Basket Pattern

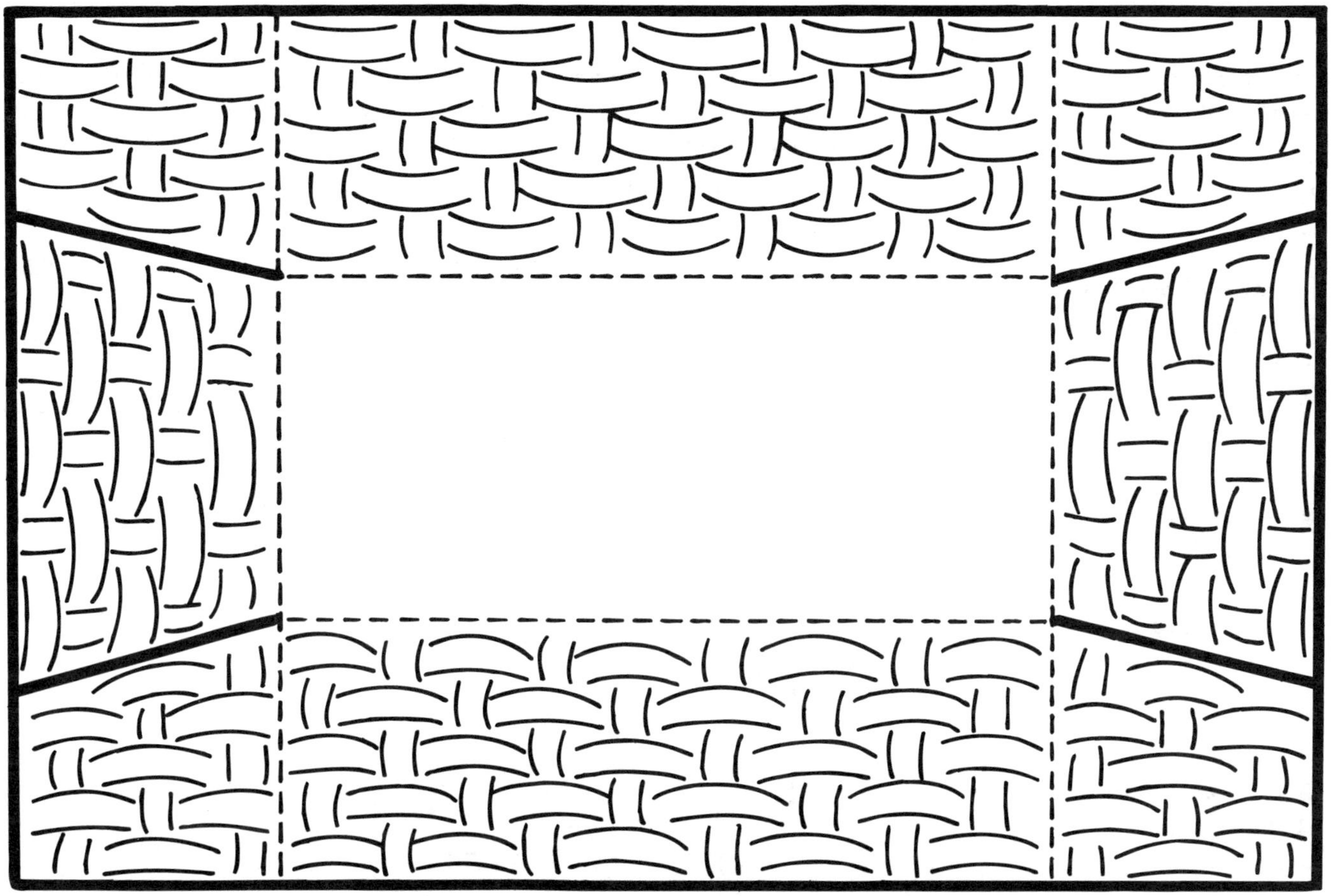

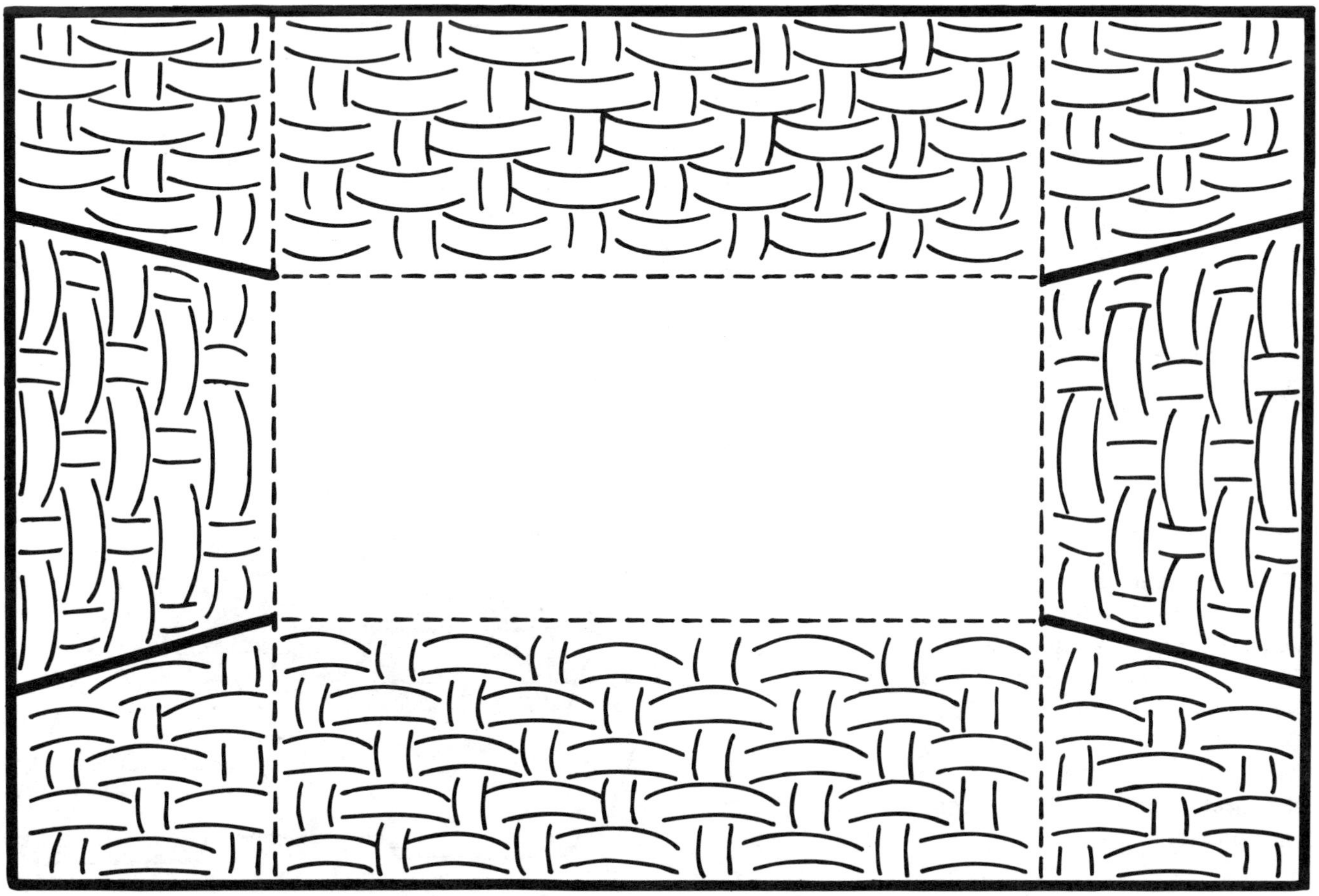

My Own Computer (15-20 MINUTES)

Materials

- Keyboard Pattern (p. 31)
- Screen Patterns (p. 32)
- star or space-themed stickers

For every two children—

- 9x12-inch (23x30.5-cm) sheet craft foam
- two letter-sized file folders in bright colors

Optional—

- SonForce Assortment stickers (available from Gospel Light)

Standard Supplies

- scissors
- ruler
- craft knife
- white card stock
- stapler
- crayons or markers

Preparation

Cut craft foam sheets in half to make one 6x9-inch (15x23-cm) rectangle for each child. Use craft knife to cut a 4x6½-inch (10x16.5-cm) window in each rectangle (sketch a). Photocopy onto card stock one Keyboard Pattern and one set of Screen Patterns for each child. Cut out all patterns. Trace a Screen Pattern onto additional card stock and cut out to make one or more blank Screen Patterns for each child.

Conversation

What message is on your computer screen? What are some ways you can help others at VBS, Corinne? When we help others, we are showing our love for God. Our Bible says, *With love, help each other* (Galatians 5:13). **Let's say that together.** Repeat verse with children.

Instruct each child in the following procedures:

- Use stickers and crayons or markers to decorate front of file folders.
- Color Keyboard Pattern.
- Color Keyboard and Screen Patterns and/or draw and color on blank Screen Patterns.
- With teacher's help, staple screen frame to inside top of folder to make a pocket (sketch b).
- With teacher's help, staple Keyboard Pattern to inside bottom of folder to make another pocket (sketch b).
- Slide one Screen Pattern behind screen frame. Store your additional Screen Patterns in the pocket behind the keyboard.

a.

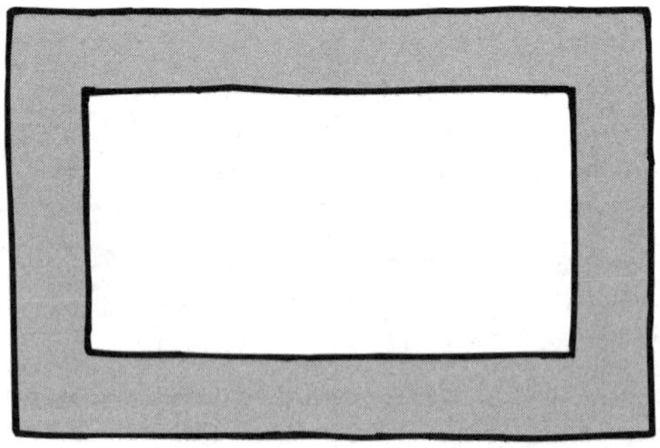

b.

Keyboard Pattern

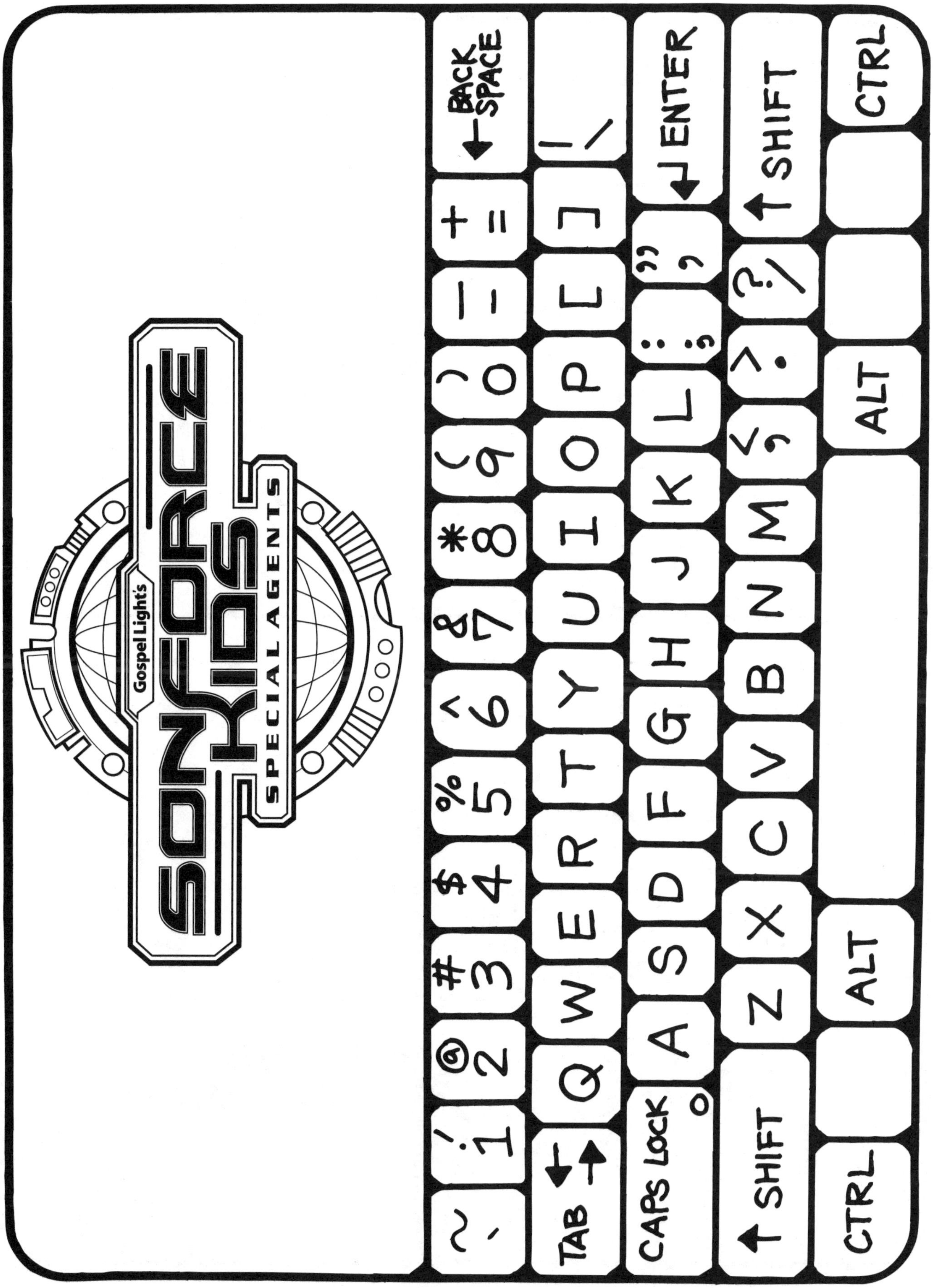

"Trust in the Lord." (See Jeremiah 17:7.)

"With love, help each other." Galatians 5:13

Windsock Comet *(15–20 MINUTES)*

Materials

- construction paper in various colors
- wide metallic gift-wrapping ribbon
- yarn
- gold and silver ink pads
- star-shaped stamps
- glitter pens

For each child—

- 12x18-inch (30.5x45.5-cm) sheet of black construction paper
- 1-inch (2.5-cm) metal washer

Standard Supplies

- scissors
- measuring stick
- glue
- stapler

Preparation

Cut the construction paper into two 18x1-inch (45.5x2.5-cm) strips for each child. Cut wide ribbon into 10 to 12 12-inch (30.5-cm) lengths for each child. Cut yarn into two 18-inch (45.5-cm) lengths for each child. Tie a knot at the end of each length of yarn.

Conversation

Mia, your windsock has many pretty colors! Thank you for giving Diana some of the silver ribbon. You are obeying God when you share with others. Our Bible says, *Obey me, and I will be your God* (Jeremiah 7:23)**. Let's say our verse together.** Lead children to repeat verse.

Instruct each child in the following procedures:

- Use star stamps and glitter pens to decorate black construction paper.
- Squeeze a line of glue along one long edge of your paper. Lay one construction-paper strip on glue, matching edges (sketch a).
- On opposite edge of paper, squeeze another line of glue. Press one end of each piece of ribbon onto glue, leaving a little space between ribbons. Continue adding ribbon until edge is evenly covered (sketch b).
- Lay the second construction-paper strip over ends of ribbons, matching edges of black paper (sketch c).
- With teacher's help, shape paper into a tube and staple edges together (sketch d).
- With teacher's help, staple knotted ends of yarn to each side of the end of your tube and tie opposite ends of yarn to washer (sketch d).

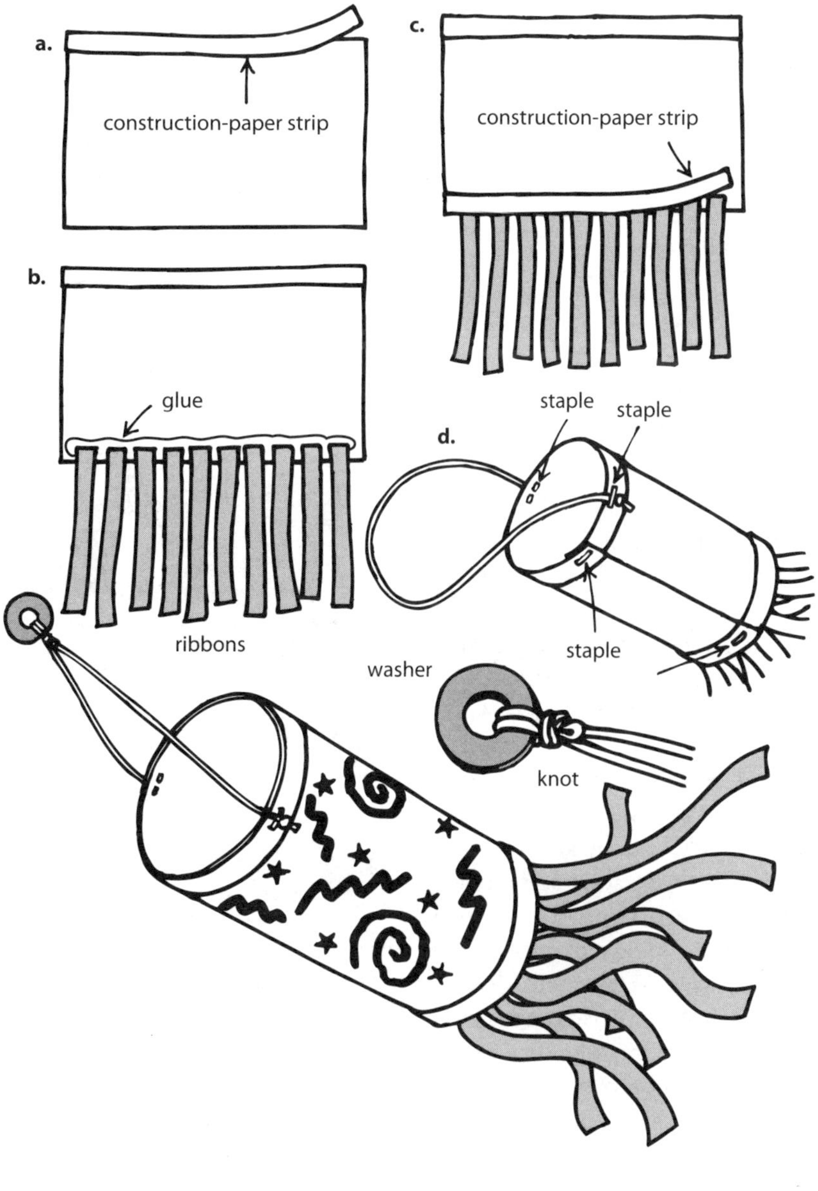

SonForce Gadget Belt (15-20 MINUTES)

Materials

- Gadget Patterns (p. 35)
- waxed paper
- fabric scissors
- glitter felt or hi-tech print fabric (neon colors, abstract designs)
- sewing machine
- white thread
- large safety pin
- neon or metallic colored pens or fabric paints in various colors

For each child—

- 3-foot (.9-m) shoelace in neon or metallic color
- two tongue depressors
- child-sized scissors

Standard Supplies

- ruler
- white card stock
- scissors
- crayons or markers

Preparation

Cut waxed paper into two 5-inch (12.5-cm) squares for each child. Photocopy one set of Gadget Patterns onto card stock for each child and cut out.

Make a Gadget Belt for each child: Cut a 10x12-inch (25.5x30.5-cm) rectangle of fabric. Sew a ½-inch (1.3-cm) hem on both short sides and one long side of fabric (sketch a). Fold up the hemmed long side of fabric to make a 4-inch (10-cm) pocket as shown in sketch b. Sew pocket along sides; then stitch down the middle of pocket to make two smaller pockets. Fold down ¾ inch (1.9 cm) of top edge of apron and sew along edge to make a casing. Pin safety pin to one end of shoelace and thread through casing (sketch c). Remove pin.

Instruct each child in the following procedures:

- Slide a piece of waxed paper into each pocket of belt.
- Use pens or paint in squeeze bottles to decorate pockets of belt with stars, swirls and dots (sketch d). Allow to dry.
- Using crayons or markers, color Gadget Patterns.
- Glue a tongue depressor to the back of each gadget to make it stiff (sketch e).
- Place gadgets in pockets of belt.

Enrichment Idea

Older children use neon or metallic pens to write "SonForce" on pockets of belt. Give children party-favor flashlights and other gadgets to keep in tool belts.

a.

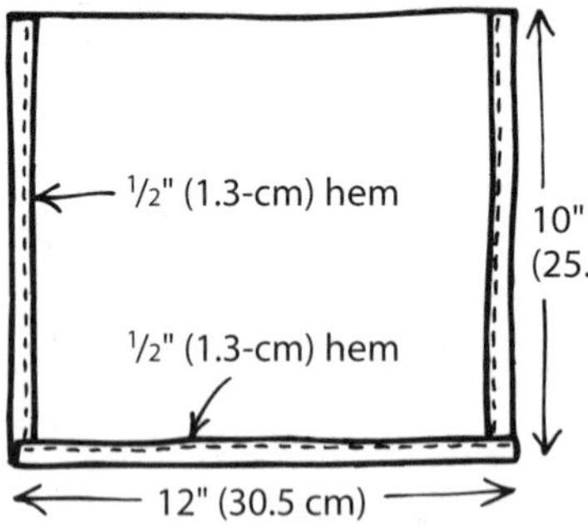

b.

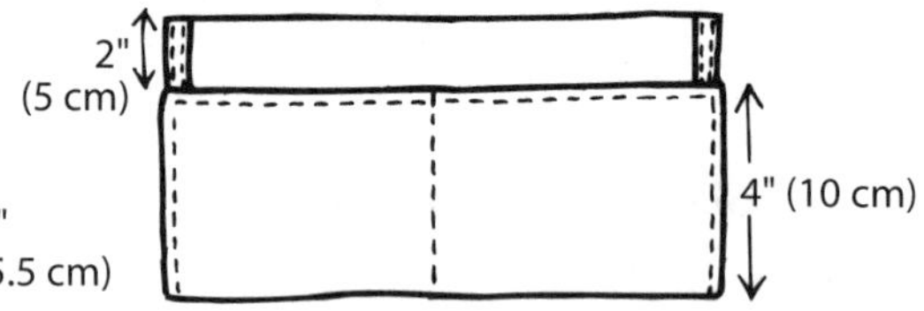

front of belt

c.

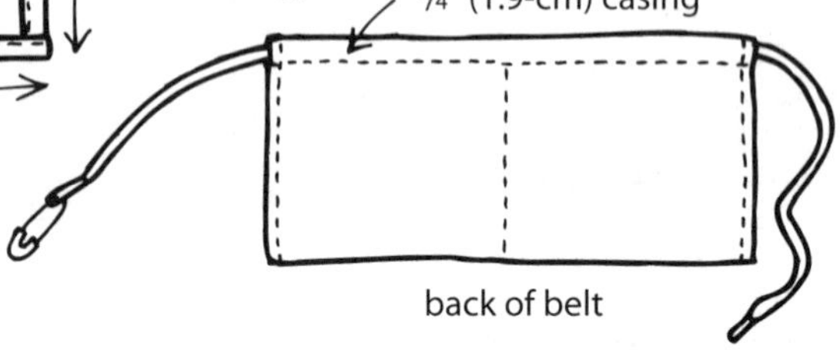

back of belt

d.

e.

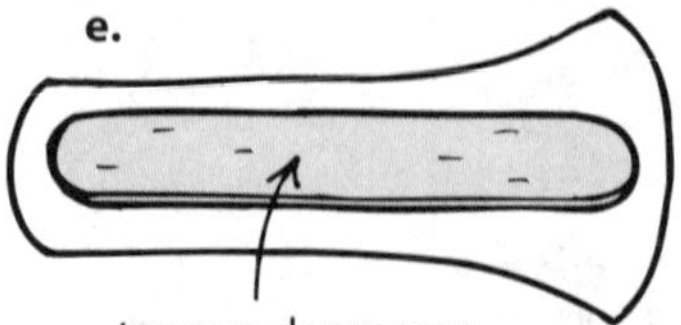

tongue depressor

Conversation

Flashlights help us to be able to see when it is dark. Lily, when have you used a flashlight? Our Bible says, ***Trust in the Lord*** (see Jeremiah 17:7)**. You can trust that God is always with you. He is with you when it is dark and when it is light. When you trust someone, you believe what he or she says. When we trust God, it means that we believe what He says in His Word, the Bible.**

Gadget Patterns

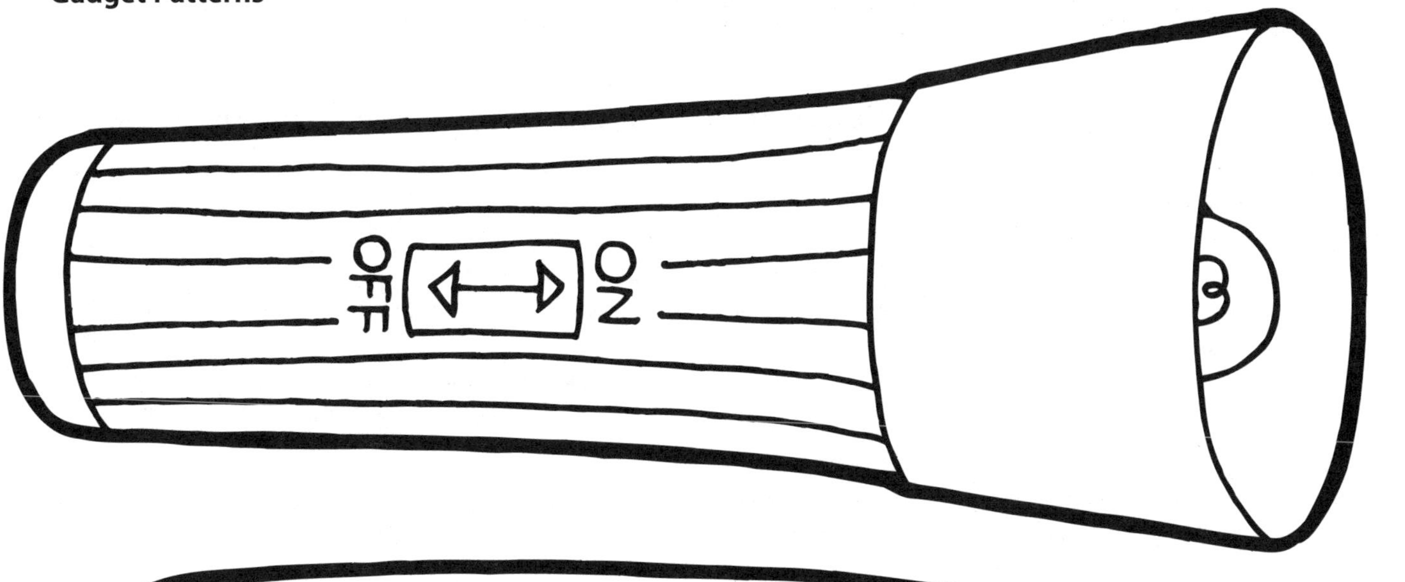

Jeremiah's Scroll (15-20 MINUTES)

Materials

- ribbon in various colors
- gold or brown craft paint
- wide-tip permanent markers in various colors
- felt stickers in various shapes (or precut shapes from felt scraps—stars, hearts, circles, triangles, flowers)

For each child—

- two wooden paint-stirring sticks
- 10x18-inch (25.5x45.5-cm) piece of light-colored felt
- glittered ponytail holder

Standard Supplies

- scissors
- measuring stick
- foam paintbrush
- glue

Preparation

Cut ribbon into two 2-foot (.6-m) lengths for each child. Use foam paintbrush to paint both sides of stirring sticks brown or gold. Let dry.

Conversation

Jeremiah obeyed God when he told Baruch to write God's words on a scroll. Our Bible says, *Obey me, and I will be your God* (Jeremiah 7:23). **Obeying God means you do what God's Word says. Cole, what did you share with Ethan? When you shared the pens with Ethan, you were obeying God's Word. Thank you.**

Instruct each child in the following procedures:

- Glue sticks to sides of felt piece so that handle ends are at the bottom (sketch a).
- Use markers to color designs on felt.
- Peel and stick (or glue) felt shapes onto felt piece.
- With teacher's help, tie a piece of ribbon to the handle of each stick (sketch b).
- When dry, roll the ends of your scroll until they meet in the middle. With teacher's help, slide ponytail holder around rolled-up scroll (sketch c).

Enrichment Idea

Older children use markers to write the words "Jeremiah Obeyed God" on their scrolls. They paint their own stirring sticks and let dry while decorating felt.

Budget Tips

Children use brown-paper grocery bags to make scrolls. Cut bags into 10x18-inch (25.5x45.5-cm) pieces. To give bags a leather-like look, children crumple and un-crumple several times and then smooth out. Instead of ponytail holders, use a length of ribbon to tie scrolls closed.

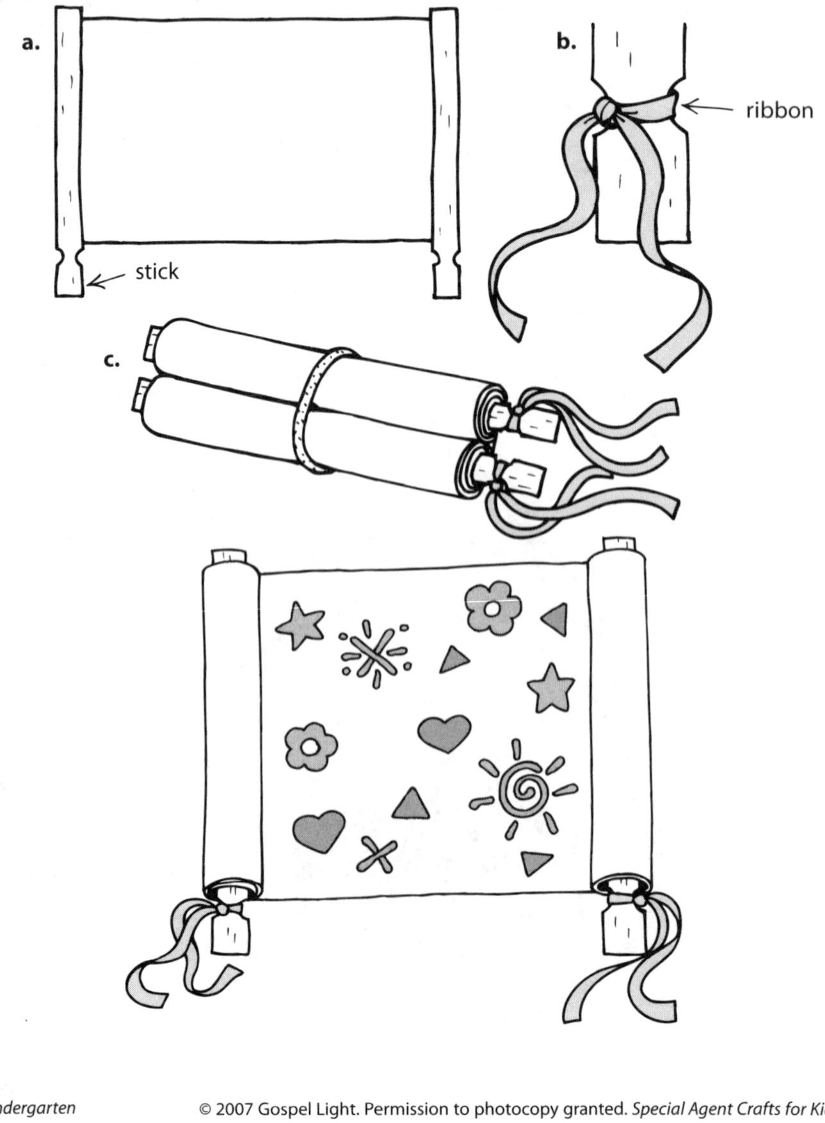

Catch a Falling Star (15-20 MINUTES)

Materials

- blow-dryer
- colored electrical tape
- metallic yarn
- aluminum foil
- silver curling ribbon
- space stickers

For each child—

- 2-liter soda bottle
- pony bead
- 2-inch (5-cm) Styrofoam ball

Standard Supplies

- craft knife
- scissors
- measuring stick
- ballpoint pens
- craft glue

Preparation

Rinse bottles. Remove labels. (If needed, use blow-dryer to soften glue and easily remove labels from bottles.) Use craft knife to cut ends off of bottles. Fold lengths of tape over cut ends to cover any sharp edges (sketch a). Cut yarn into one 24-inch (61-cm) length for each child. Tie a pony bead to one end of each yarn length. Cut foil into one 8-inch (20.5-cm) square for each child. Cut curling ribbon into six 12-inch (30.5-cm) lengths for each child. Tie ends of each group of six ribbons together and knot (sketch b). Trim ends of ribbon just above knot.

Conversation

Our Bible says, ***Trust in the Lord*** (see Jeremiah 17:7)**. We can trust that God will always love us. And we can show His love to others! Evan, when you share the ribbons you are showing God's love. What are some other ways that you can show God's love?** (Use kind words. Invite others to play. Share my toy cars.)

Instruct each child in the following procedures:

- Use pen to poke a ½-inch (1.3-cm) deep hole into Styrofoam ball.
- Attach yarn length to ball by squeezing a small amount of glue into hole and pushing pony bead into hole (sketch c).
- Use pen to poke another ½-inch (1.3-cm) deep hole into Styrofoam ball at opposite end (sketch d).
- Squeeze a small amount of glue into hole and push in knot of ribbon (sketch e).
- Wrap foil square around ball to make falling star (sketch f). Let glue dry.
- Decorate bottles with space stickers.
- Unscrew bottle cap and thread approximately 4 inches (10 cm) of yarn tip through bottle neck. Tape tip to inside of bottle and screw lid back on.
- To play with Falling Star toy, hold bottle in one hand, flip falling star up and try to catch it inside bottle.

Simplification Idea

Children use gallon milk jugs instead of 2-liter bottles. Before class, use a craft knife to cut away bottom of jug. Wrap cut edges with tape. Children decorate jugs with stickers and then, with teacher's help, tie falling stars onto handles. Children hold the handle of jug with open end up and try to catch falling star in bottom of jug.

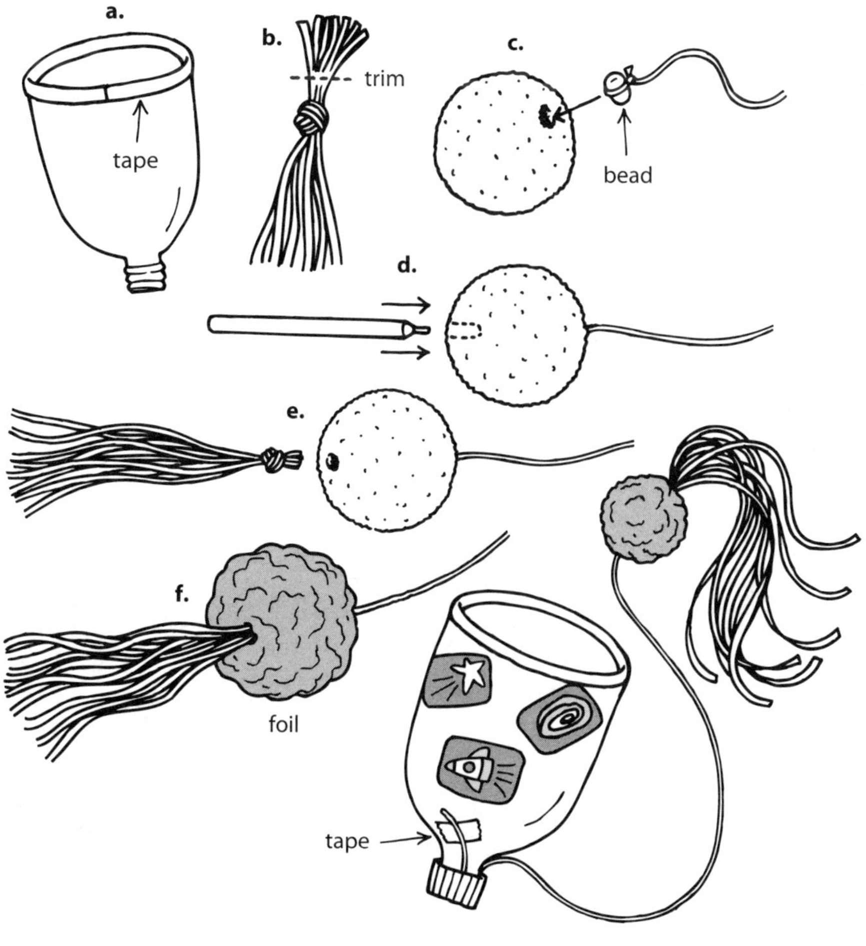

Veggie Concentration (15-20 MINUTES)

Materials

- Veggie Cards (p. 39)
- markers in various colors, including red, green, yellow and orange
- stickers

For each child—

- sandwich-sized resealable plastic bag

Standard Supplies

- white card stock
- scissors

Preparation

Photocopy one set of Veggie Cards onto card stock for each child.

Conversation

Tyler, thank you for listening carefully to my instructions. Daniel and his friends listened to God's instructions. They obeyed God's rules about what food to eat. Our Bible says, *Listen to advice and you will be wise* (see Proverbs 19:20). **Being wise means you know and do what is right. When you obey these words, you are being wise like Daniel.**

Instruct each child in the following procedures:

- Use markers to color Veggie Cards, making sure to color each vegetable the same color (green peas, red tomatoes, yellow corn and orange carrots).
- Cut apart Veggie Cards.
- Place stickers on resealable plastic bags.
- Use Veggie Cards to play Concentration. With a friend, arrange cards face-down. Take turns turning over two cards at a time to find matching cards. Continue playing until all pairs are collected. Repeat game as time and interest allow. When finished, store cards in resealable bags.

Enrichment Idea

Before VBS begins, collect empty seed packets. Instead of envelopes, children store cards in packets.

Veggie Cards

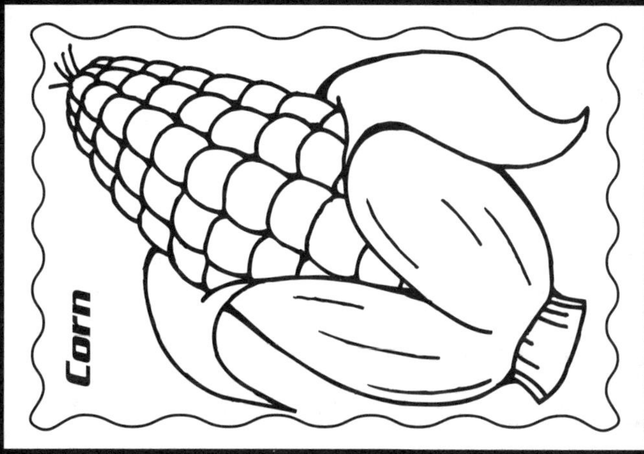

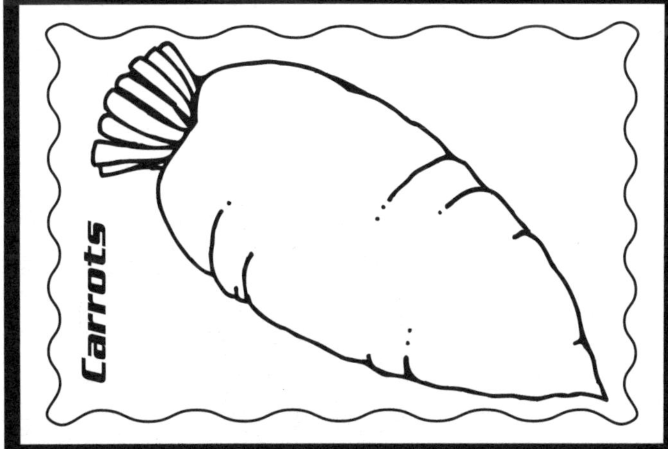

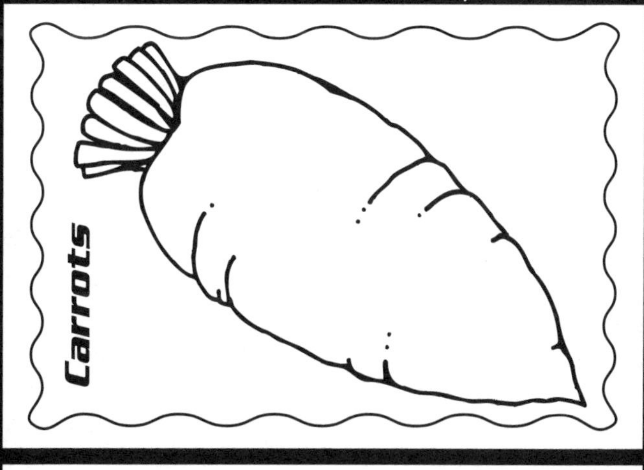

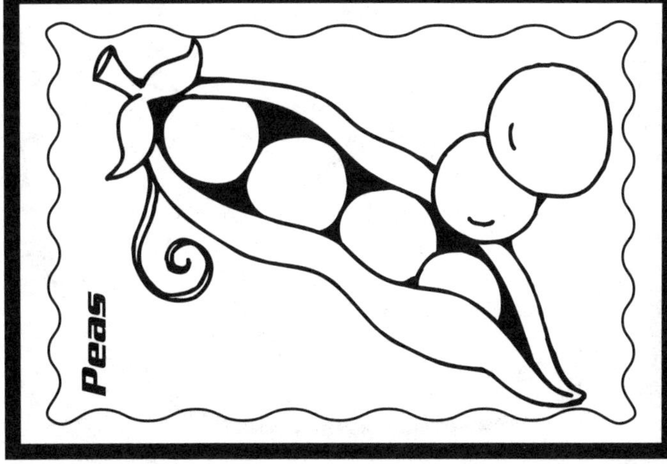

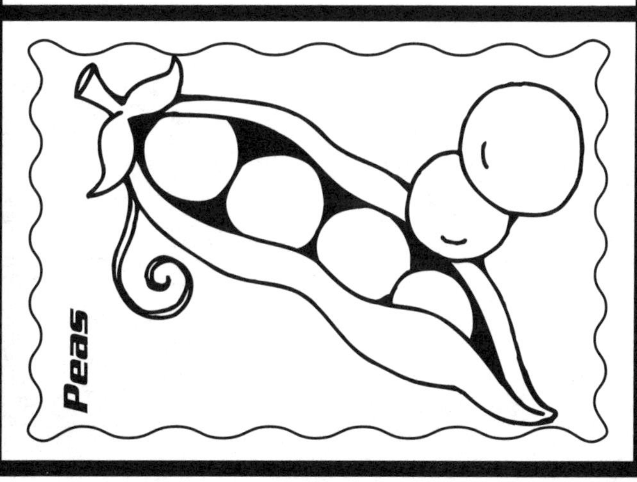

Joshua and Caleb Take a Peek

(15–20 MINUTES)

Materials

- House Pattern (p. 41)
- Joshua and Caleb Pattern (p. 40)

For each child—

- paper fastener

Standard Supplies

- white card stock
- scissors
- crayons or markers
- hole punch
- stapler

Preparation

Photocopy onto card stock one House Pattern and one Joshua and Caleb Pattern for each child. Cut out Joshua and Caleb Patterns. Fold House Pattern along lines 1 and 2 and cut slots in line 1 (sketch a). Unfold so it lays flat. Use the point of scissors to pierce a hole at the *X* on front of House Pattern.

Instruct each child in the following procedures:

- Use crayons or markers to color Joshua, Caleb and house.
- With teacher's help, punch a hole in the dot on the Joshua and Caleb Pattern.
- Insert Joshua and Caleb Pattern into slots cut in line 1 (sketch b).
- With teacher's help, insert paper fastener through hole in House Pattern and then through hole in Joshua and Caleb Pattern (sketch c).
- Staple top and bottom of House Pattern (sketch d).
- Gently press down on tab with arrow to make Joshua and Caleb peek out from behind building.

Enrichment Ideas

Children cut out their own Joshua and Caleb Patterns. Provide cotton balls to glue on card for sky. Children spread a thin layer of glue on House and sprinkle sand over glue to give building texture.

Conversation

God was with Joshua and Caleb when they explored the Promised Land. Our Bible says, *Be strong and courageous . . . for the Lord your God will be with you wherever you go* (Joshua 1:9). **God is with you wherever you go. Even when we feel afraid, God will help us. Where are some places you like to go, Hannah? God is with you when you go there!**

a.

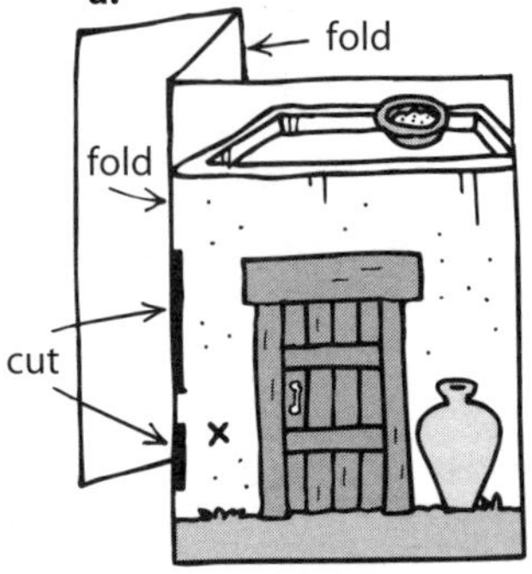

b.

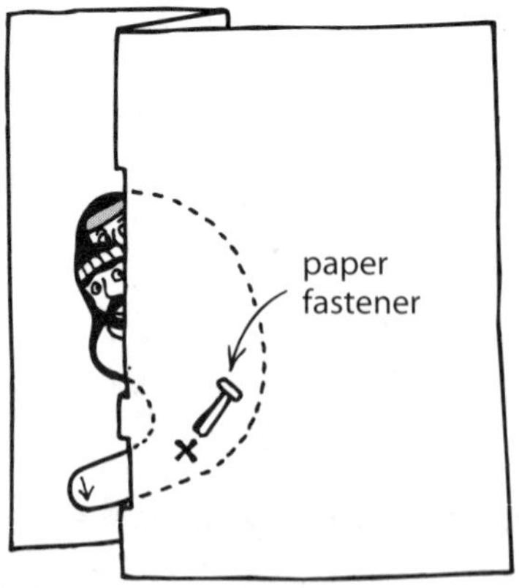

c.

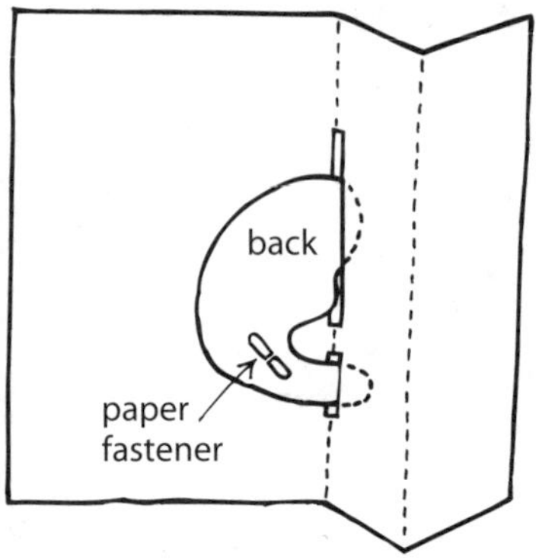

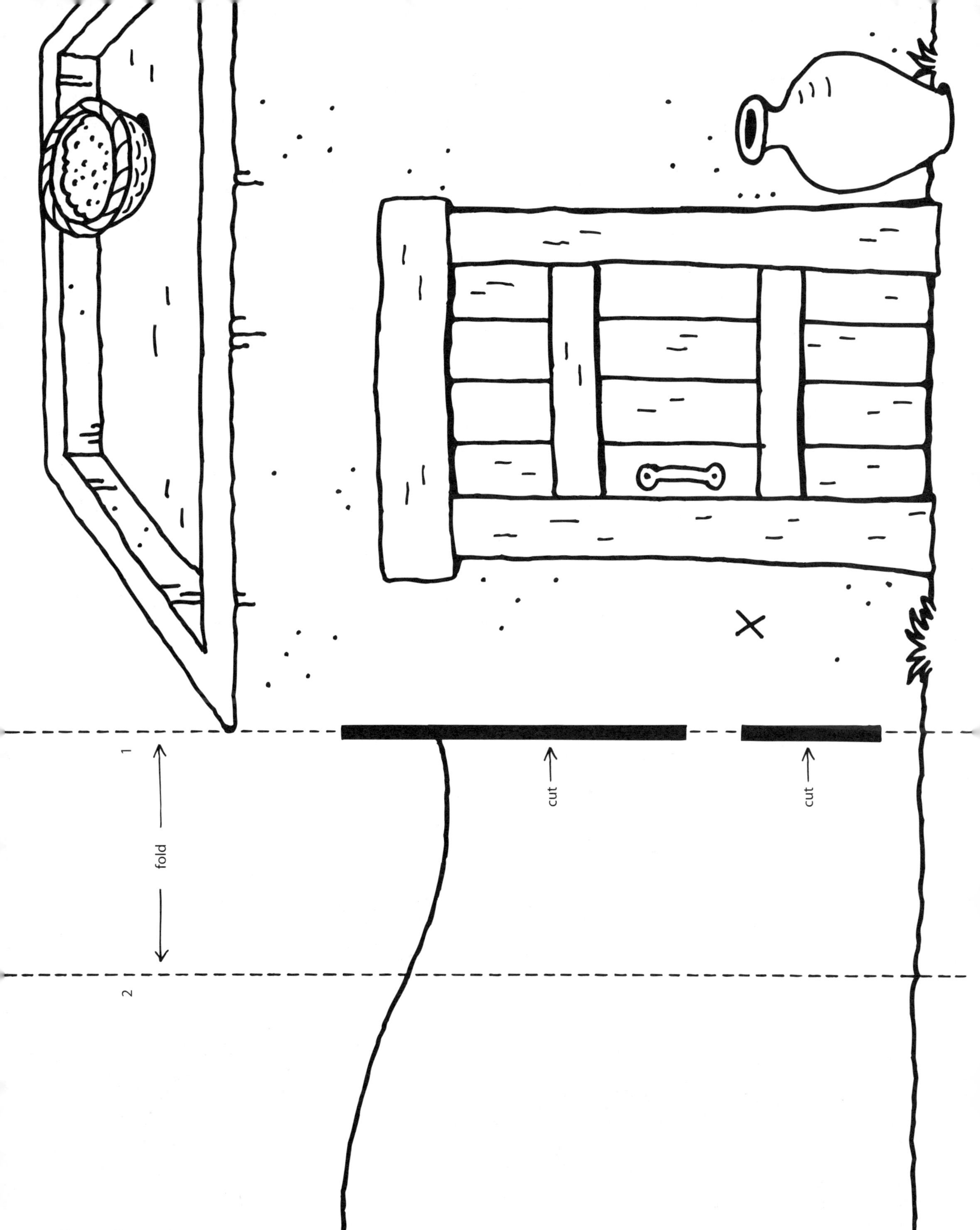

House Pattern

Starry, Starry Light Gift

(TWO-DAY CRAFT/35–40 MINUTES TOTAL TIME)

Materials

- tissue paper in various colors
- foil star stickers
- glitter

For each child—

- baby-food jar
- tea light

Standard Supplies

- newspaper
- craft glue
- shallow containers
- scissors
- ruler
- paintbrushes

DAY ONE Preparation

Cover work area with newspaper. Pour glue into shallow containers and dilute with water. Cut tissue paper into approximately 2-inch (5-cm) squares.

Instruct each child in the following procedures:

- With paintbrush, spread a coat of glue over a small area of the outside of the jar. Apply a square of tissue and brush with glue again (sketch a).
- Continue applying tissue squares, overlapping as you go, until outside of jar is covered. With teacher's help, at the bottom edge of jar, turn tissue edges under (sketch b) and brush with diluted glue. Let jar dry overnight.

DAY TWO Preparation

Pour glue into shallow containers and dilute with water. Pour glitter into shallow container. Cover work area with newspaper.

Instruct each child in the following procedures:

- Put star stickers over the tissue-paper squares (sketch c).
- Brush a thin layer of diluted glue over entire jar and then roll lightly in glitter. Let dry.
- Put tea light into jar.
- Give your Starry, Starry Light Gift to someone you love!

Enrichment Idea

Instead of covering jars with tissue paper, children put foil stars on baby-food jars. They paint over stars with gold-colored paint. When dry, children pull off star stickers, revealing star shapes on jars.

a.

b.

Conversation

Morgan, you moved over to give Ally room to put glitter on her jar. Thank you. You are a kind friend! Our Bible says, *With love help each other* (Galatians 5:13)**. You are showing God's love when you are kind and help others. What are some other ways that you can be kind at VBS? At home?**

c.

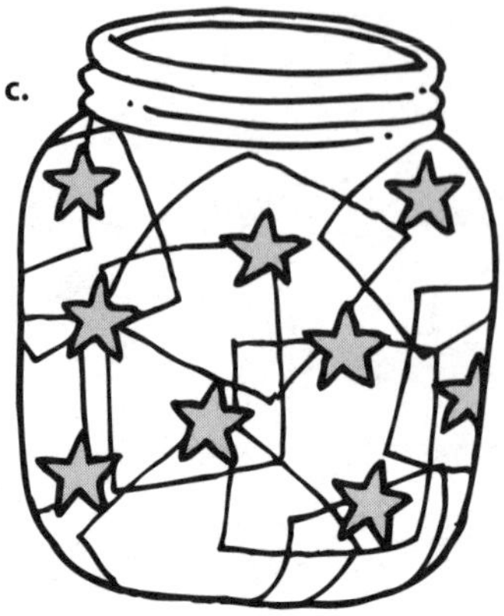

SECTION TWO

Grades 1–3

Crafts for Younger Elementary

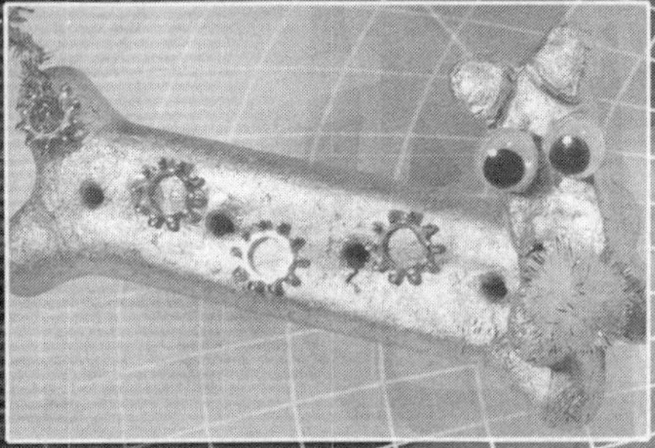

Children in the first few years of school delight in completing craft projects. They have a handle on most of the basic skills needed, they are eager to participate and their taste in art has usually not yet surpassed their ability to produce. In other words, they generally like what they make.

Because reading ability is not a factor in most craft projects, crafts can be a great leveler among children. Some children who are not top achievers in other areas excel here.

You may find additional projects suitable for younger elementary children in the first section of this book, "Crafts for Young Children."

SonForce Agent Badge (15-20 MINUTES)

Materials

- Badge, Inside Top and Inside Bottom Patterns (p. 45)
- black vinyl
- colored pencils

Optional—

- Agent Level Badges stickers (available from Gospel Light)

Standard Supplies

- scissors
- ruler
- card stock
- ballpoint pens
- craft glue

Preparation

Cut vinyl into one 4½x6-inch (11.5x 15-cm) rectangle to make a badge holder for each child. Photocopy onto card stock one set of Badge, Inside Top and Inside Bottom Patterns for each child.

Conversation

Special agents carry badges that tell who they are and what agency they work for. Before being given a badge, the agents must promise to carry out the missions that they were trained for. Your SonForce Agent Badges tell the five missions of a SonForce agent. Ricky, what does it mean to "TRUST in God's Plans"? (Believe that God loves you and that His plans are the best for your life.)

Instruct each child in the following procedures:

- Cut out all patterns.
- On the Inside Bottom Pattern, write your name and a badge number, and sign your name. Color the five "level badge" circles. (Optional: Place an Agent Level Badges sticker over each circle.)
- Fold badge holder in half and glue on Badge Pattern as shown in sketch a.
- Unfold badge holder and turn over. Glue on Inside Top and Inside Bottom Patterns as shown in sketch b. (Note: Check to be sure that inside of badge will not be upside down when badge is opened.)
- At home, glue a photo of yourself to the Inside Top Pattern of badge. (Optional: Instead of using a photo, draw a picture of yourself.)

Simplification Idea

For younger children, precut badges before class begins.

Enrichment Idea

One or two days prior to this craft, use a digital camera to photograph and print a picture of each child. (Note: Pictures will be glued to Inside Top Pattern of badge, so size accordingly.)

Budget Tip

Make badge holders out of black sparkle felt or craft foam. If using sparkle felt, glue two pieces back to back for a sturdier craft. If using craft foam, prefold each badge holder and score both sides of fold several times with the end of a paper clip.

a.

b.

Inside Top Pattern

As a Special Agent of SonForce Kids, this agent promises to:
TRUST in God's plans,
UNITE with God's people,
TRAIN for God's service,
FOLLOW in God's path and
LEAD others to God's promises.

Agent Name: ______________________

Badge No.: ______________________

Signature: ______________________

Be strong and courageous . . . for the Lord your God will be with you wherever you go. Joshua 1:9

LEVEL 1 LEVEL 2 LEVEL 3 LEVEL 4 LEVEL 5

Inside Bottom Pattern

Inside Top Pattern

As a Special Agent of SonForce Kids, this agent promises to:
TRUST in God's plans,
UNITE with God's people,
TRAIN for God's service,
FOLLOW in God's path and
LEAD others to God's promises.

Agent Name: ______________________

Badge No.: ______________________

Signature: ______________________

Be strong and courageous . . . for the Lord your God will be with you wherever you go. Joshua 1:9

LEVEL 1 LEVEL 2 LEVEL 3 LEVEL 4 LEVEL 5

Inside Bottom Pattern

Badge Pattern

Badge Pattern

Rocket Bookmark (15-20 MINUTES)

Materials

- Rocket Pattern (p. 46)
- clear Con-Tact paper
- embroidery floss in red, orange and/or yellow
- large bamboo skewers
- scratch-art paper (available at art-supply stores)

Standard Supplies

- card stock
- scissors
- rulers
- hole punch

Preparation

Photocopy onto card stock one Rocket Pattern for every three children and cut out. Cut clear Con-Tact paper into two 4x8-inch (10x20.5-cm) rectangles for each child. Cut five 12-inch (30.5-cm) lengths of floss for each child.

Conversation

What words did you write on your bookmark, Corinne? When are some times you can show that you trust God? The Bible says, *Blessed is the man who trusts in the Lord, whose confidence is in him* (Jeremiah 17:7)**. When you believe in God's love and plans for you, it gives you courage to trust Him in every situation.**

Instruct each child in the following procedures:

- Use skewer to trace Rocket Pattern onto scratch-art paper and cut out.
- Use skewer to scratch words and designs onto your rocket.
- With teacher's help, peel the backing off one piece of clear Con-Tact paper. Press your rocket shape, decorated side down, onto center of sticky side.
- Peel the backing off second piece of clear Con-Tact paper. Press over back of rocket shape. Trim edges of Con-Tact paper.
- Punch hole at bottom of rocket (sketch a).
- Thread four lengths of floss through hole until hole is at center of floss. Fold floss over, matching ends (sketch b).
- Tie a fifth length of floss around the folded floss on rocket and trim long ends to make a tassel, representing rocket-engine flames (sketch b).

Budget Tip

Children make their own scratch-art paper. They use crayons to color paper rectangles in patches of bright color. Then children use a black crayon to color over the top of bright colors.

b.

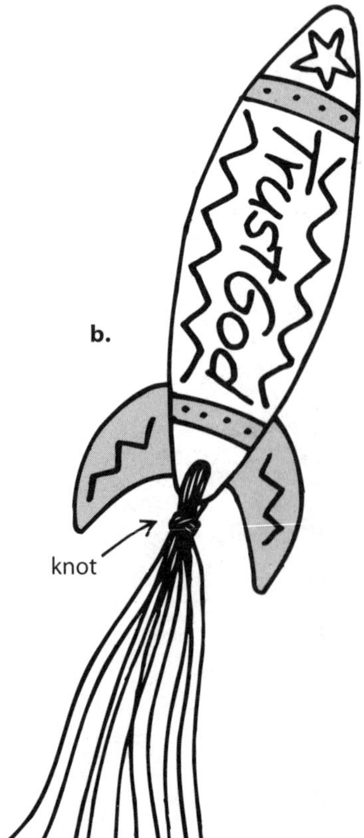

a.

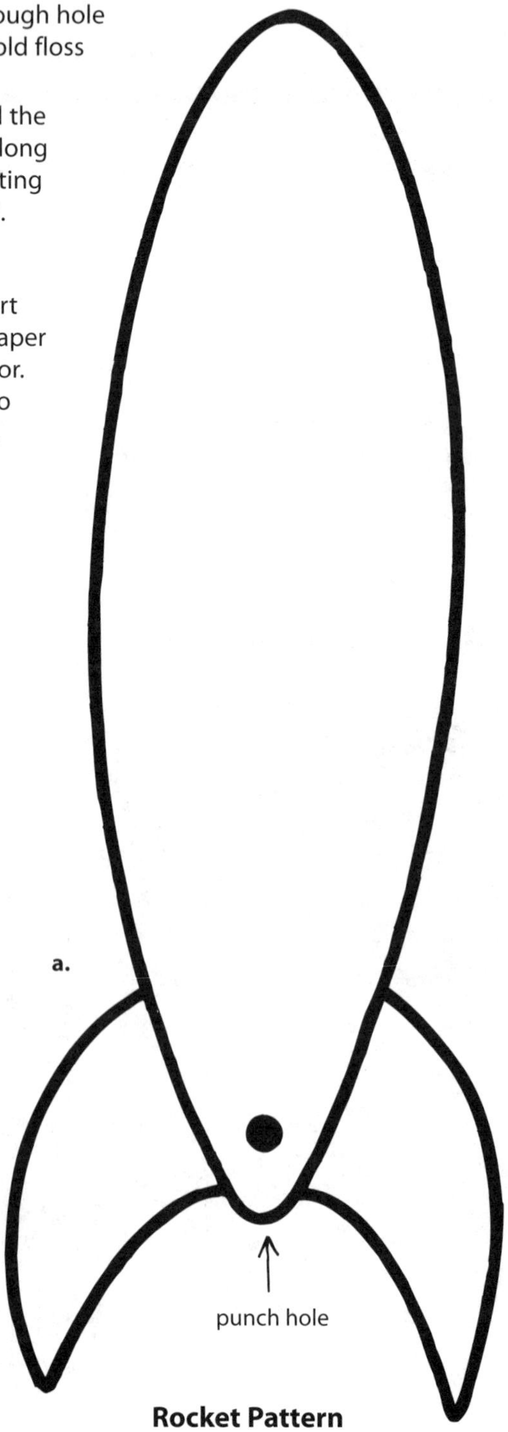

Rocket Pattern

Global Compass System (GCS)

(15-20 MINUTES)

Materials

- Wristband Pattern (p. 47)
- craft foam in various colors
- glitter glue or acrylic paint in various neon colors
- toothpicks

For each child—

- 1-inch (2.5-cm) square of self-adhesive Velcro
- small plastic compass

Standard Supplies

- scissors or pinking shears
- permanent marker
- craft glue

Preparation

Trace Wristband Pattern onto craft foam and cut out to make one wristband for each child. Mark a dot on each wristband with permanent marker as shown on pattern.

Conversation

A compass is a good tool to carry when you are out walking. It can keep you from getting lost and help you when you need directions. Where are some places you go that you could use your compass, Miguel? The Bible says, *Be strong and courageous . . . for the Lord your God will be with you wherever you go* (Joshua 1:9). **God loves us. We can believe God when He tells us that He is always with us.**

Instruct each child in the following procedures:

- Peel the backing off one half of Velcro and stick at one end of the Wristband Pattern.
- Turn wristband over and peel and stick the other half of Velcro to opposite end of wristband.
- Squeeze glue onto the dot on your wristband.
- With the *N* on your compass pointing to one end of your wristband, press the compass onto the glue (sketch a).
- Squeeze six to eight large dots of paint onto your wristband.
- Use the tip of a toothpick to spread the paint out in splatter or squiggle designs (sketch b). Let dry.
- To fasten wristband to your wrist, press Velcro pieces together. The *N* should be at the top when you look at your compass.

Enrichment Idea

Take children on a walk. Using compasses, ask the children to identify which direction they are facing as they walk.

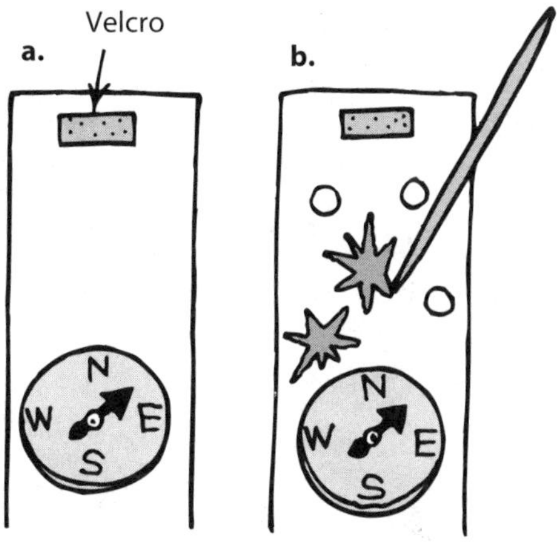

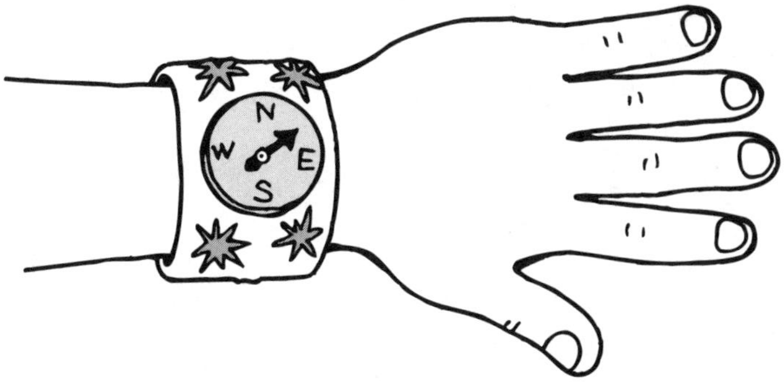

Wristband Pattern

Comet Launcher (20-25 MINUTES)

Materials

- brightly colored electrical or duct tape
- brightly colored stickers in geometric shapes
- metallic curling ribbon

For every 12 children—

- 8-foot (2.4-m) clear, fluorescent light-bulb guard (available on the Internet or at hardware stores)

For each child—

- 1½-inch bouncy ball
- 1x24-inch (2.5x61-cm) strip of red or yellow lightweight knit fabric

Standard Supplies

- scissors
- measuring stick
- card stock

Preparation

Use scissors to cut light-bulb guard into one 8-inch (20.5-cm) length of tube for each child. Cut tape into 4 to 6-inch (10-15-cm) lengths to make six lengths of electrical tape or three lengths of duct tape for each child. (Hint: Hang tape pieces along table or counter edge so that children can easily remove them when needed.) Cut card stock into one 1¼-inch (3-cm) circle for each child.

Conversation

Comets are big pieces of ice and dust that travel through space. Sometimes they come close enough to Earth that we can see them. Where will you fly your comet, Gabriel? God loves you. No matter where you are, God is with you. Our Bible says, *Be strong and courageous . . . for the Lord your God will be with you wherever you go* (Joshua 1:9)**.**

Instruct each child in the following procedures:

- Stick card-stock circle onto middle of one length of tape (sketch a).
- Place tape over one end of tube, centering card-stock circle over end of tube (sketch b).
- Smooth ends of tape around outside of tube (sketch c). Wrap other lengths of tape around bottom of tube to secure and decorate.
- Use stickers to decorate outside of tube.
- Place ball at center of fabric strip. Wrap fabric over ball. With teacher's help, tightly tie fabric with ribbon to make comet tails (sketch d).
- Place ball tail first inside tube.
- In an outdoor area, hold taped end of Comet Launcher. Swing tube over your head to launch your comet (sketch e). (Hint: Be careful not let go of the tube, or you'll launch your Launcher!)

Enrichment Ideas

On comets' tails, children use fabric markers to write Daily Missions from SonForce Kids VBS (Trust! Unite! Train! Follow! Lead!). They design their own stickers, using fine-tip markers and glitter pens to color designs onto squares of clear Con-Tact paper; they cut out stickers and place on tubes.

Budget Tip

Instead of fluorescent light-bulb guards, decorate paper-towel tubes to make Comet Launchers.

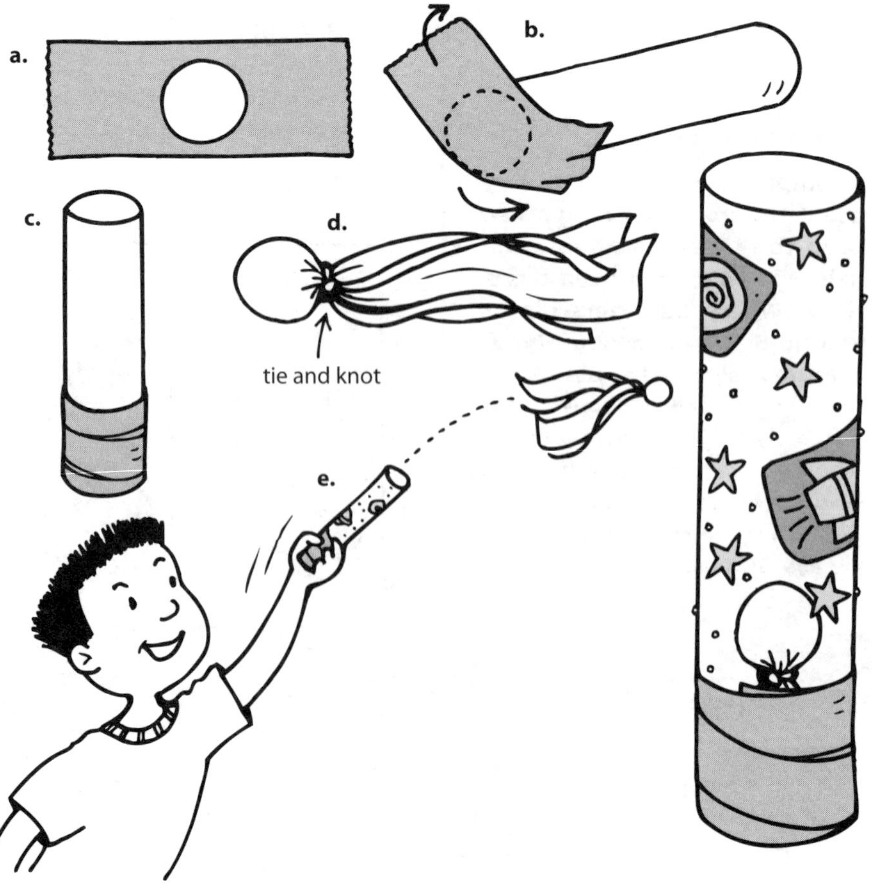

Blast-Off Rocket (20-25 MINUTES)

Materials

- Nose-cone Pattern (p. 49)
- Tail-fin Patterns (p. 49)
- card stock in various bright colors
- copier paper in various bright colors
- low-temperature glue gun

For each child—

- bendable drinking straw

Standard Supplies

- scissors
- ruler
- transparent tape
- glue

Preparation

Photocopy onto card stock one set of Nose-cone and Tail-fin Patterns for each child. Cut colored paper into one 5½x8 ½-inch (14x21.5-cm) rectangle for each child. Plug in glue gun out of reach of children.

Conversation

Emma, you listened and followed my instructions when you put your rocket together. The Bible says, ***Listen to advice and accept instruction, and in the end you will be wise*** (Proverbs 19:20). **Following God's instructions in the Bible will help you do what is right. What are some other instructions from God's Word that you can follow?** (Serve others. Pray every day. Tell the truth.)

Instruct each child in the following procedures:

- Roll paper rectangle around your straw, starting at short end of paper (sketch a). Tape edge of paper to secure (sketch b).
- Remove straw and then tape one end of paper tube closed (sketch b).
- Cut out nose cone and tail fins.
- Fold tail fins on dotted lines. Tape tail fins to one end of rocket (sketch c).
- Overlap straight edges on nose cone. Tape overlapped edge closed to form a cone (sketch d).
- With teacher's help, use glue gun to glue nose cone to top edge of rocket tube.
- Bend straw to make a square corner. Slide tube of rocket over long end of straw. Blow on short end of straw to launch rocket.

Enrichment Ideas

Use a bicycle tire pump attached to straw to launch rockets outside. Children make more than one rocket and use markers to decorate cones.

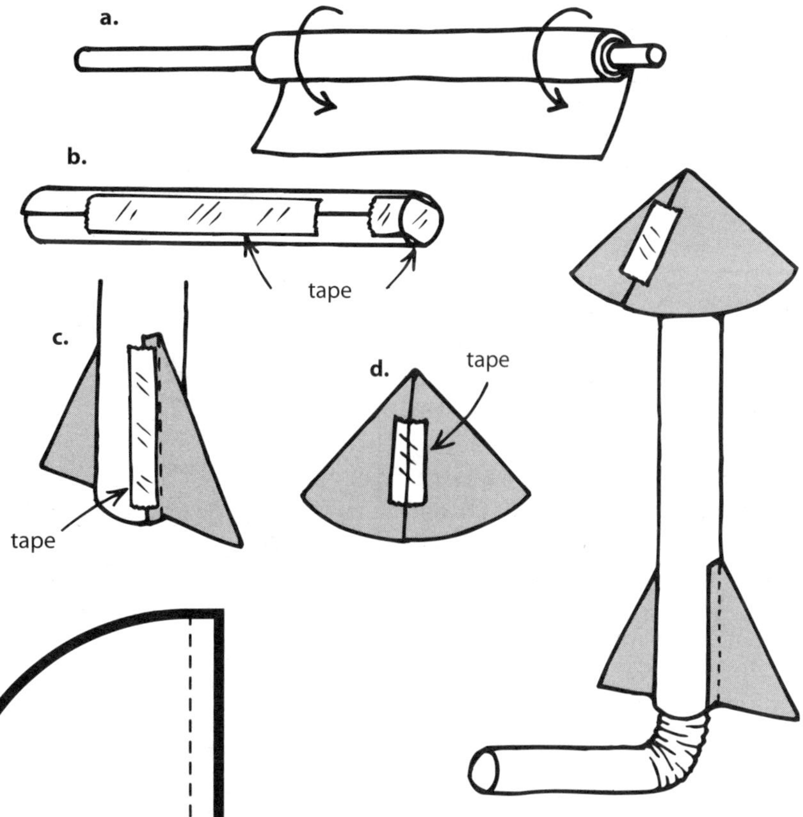

Tail-fin Patterns

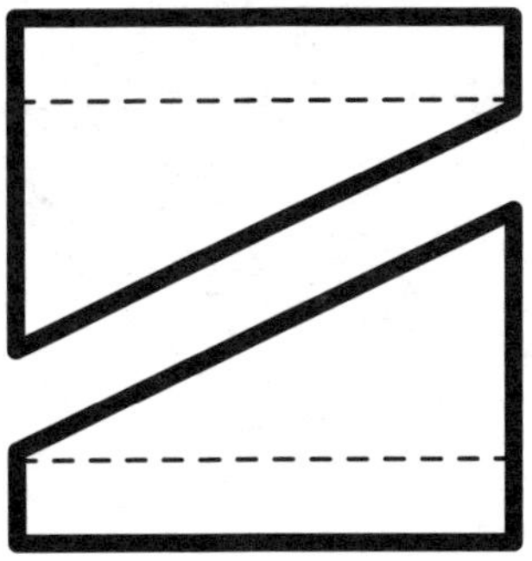

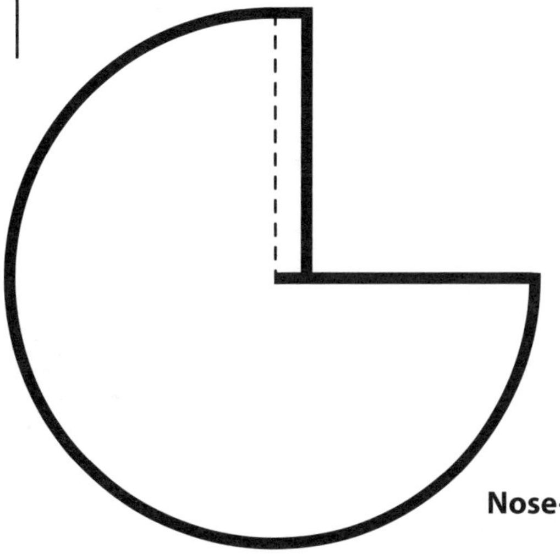

Nose-cone Pattern

Pocket Computer (20-25 MINUTES)

Materials

- Small Keyboard Pattern (p. 51)
- Computer Cover Pattern (p. 51)
- colored pencils
- fine-tip permanent markers in various colors
- inkpads
- double-stick transparent tape

For each child—

- plastic CD case
- two or three blank CDs

Standard Supplies

- card stock
- scissors

Preparation

Photocopy onto card stock one Small Keyboard Pattern and one Computer Cover Pattern for each child.

Conversation

Your Pocket Computer can help you remember the promises God gives us in the Bible. Joshua 1:9 says, *Be strong and courageous . . . for the Lord your God will be with you wherever you go.* What other promises does God give us in the Bible? (God will love us, no matter what. When we're sorry for doing something wrong, He will forgive us. He will never give up on us.)

Instruct each child in the following procedures:

- Color and cut out Computer Cover Pattern.
- Carefully loosen plastic insert that holds CD. Slide Computer Cover behind insert so that SonForce logo shows on outside of CD. Top edge of pattern should be nearest the hinge (sketch a). Push insert back into place.
- Use colored pencils to color Small Keyboard Pattern. Press thumb onto inkpad and then onto Thumbprint Identification square.
- Cut out Small Keyboard and place inside CD case, opposite the holder. (sketch b). Use a piece of double-stick tape between keyboard and case to secure in place.
- Use markers to color directly onto shiny side of CDs, designing screens for your computers with SonForce Daily Missions or memory verses (sketch c).
- Press CD to inside of case so that computer screen is showing.

Enrichment Idea

Provide extra CDs for children to make additional screens.

Budget Tip

Purchase CD storage cases at a dollar store or in bulk at a discount warehouse store.

a.

b.

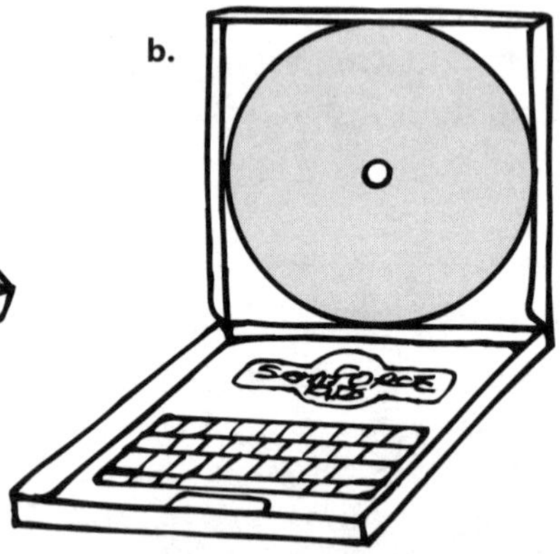

c.

Small Keyboard Pattern

Computer Cover Pattern

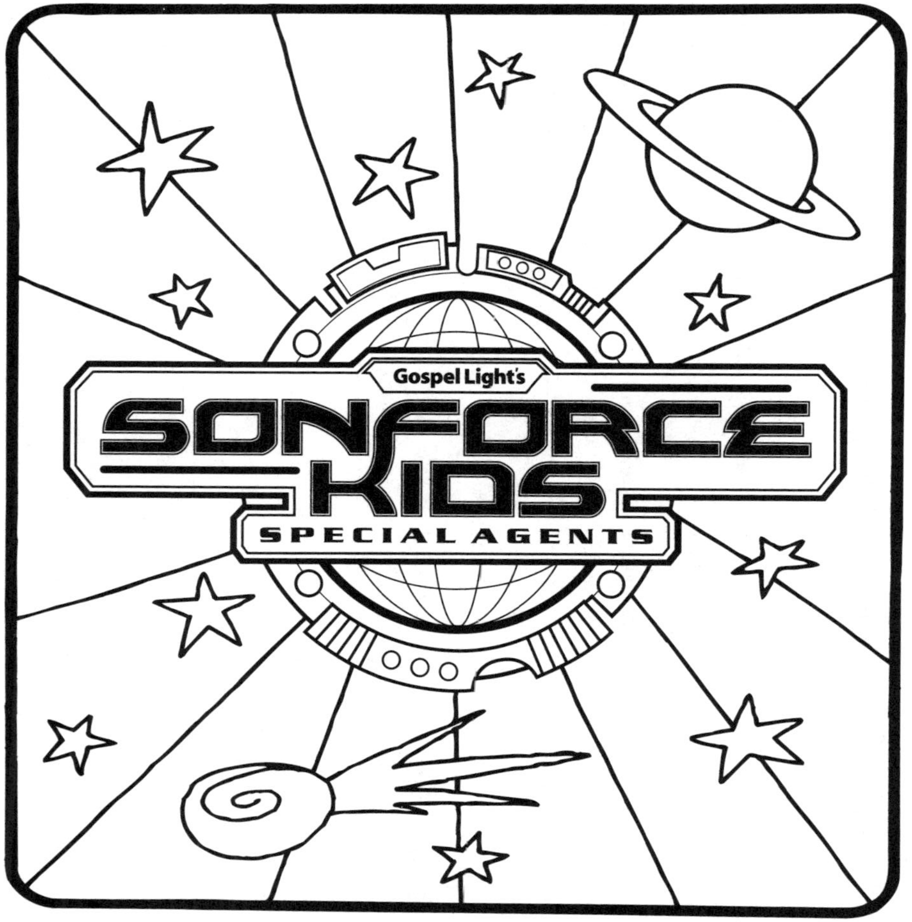

Robo-Dog (20-25 MINUTES)

Materials

- silver spray paint
- silver chenille wire
- low-temperature glue gun
- black permanent markers

For each child—

- small bone-shaped dog biscuit
- large bone-shaped dog biscuit
- two ¼-inch (.6-cm) hexagonal nuts
- two small wiggle eyes
- silver pom-pom

Standard Supplies

- newspaper
- scissors
- ruler
- craft glue
- shallow containers

Preparation

Cover outdoor work area with newspaper. Spray-paint dog biscuits silver. Let dry. Cut chenille wire into one 3-inch (7.5-cm) length for each child. Pour glue into shallow containers. Plug in glue gun out of children's reach.

Conversation

Ryan, thank you for following my directions to make your Robo-Dog. As special agents for God, it's important for us to know and follow God's directions. The Bible says, ***Walk in all the ways I command you, that it may go well with you*** (Jeremiah 7:23)**. What is a way that you will follow God's commands this week at VBS? God loves us. He wants us to follow His commands and help others to follow them, too.**

Instruct each child in the following procedures:

- With teacher's help, use glue gun to glue small dog biscuit to large one as shown in sketch a.
- Glue hexagonal nuts onto head to make dog's eyes.
- Glue wiggle eyes on top of hexagonal nuts (sketch b).
- Glue silver pom-pom onto dog's face for nose.
- Glue chenille wire onto dog for a tail.
- Use marker to draw spots on dog.

Enrichment Idea

Children glue small gears or metal washers onto dog. Instead of chenille wire they use a small spring for tail.

a.

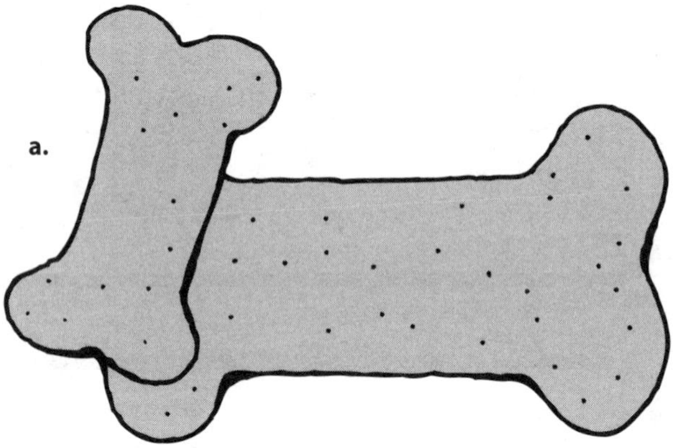

b.

Palace Ornament (20-25 MINUTES)

Materials

- metallic curling ribbon
- electrical tape
- small acrylic gems
- glitter glue
- foil star stickers

For each child—

- discarded CD

Standard Supplies

- scissors
- ruler
- glue

Preparation

Cut a 12-inch (30.5-cm) length of ribbon for each child.

Conversation

The Bible says, ***Be devoted to one another in brotherly love. Honor one another above yourselves*** (Romans 12:10)**. How did Queen Esther and her friends show love and honor to each other? Even though Esther lived in a palace with many beautiful things, she didn't just think about herself. She showed love for God by uniting with her people and helping them. What are some ways you can help others?**

Instruct each child in the following procedures:

- Tie ends of ribbon together to make a hanger. Tape knotted end of hanger onto label side of CD as shown in sketch.
- Glue acrylic gems and use glitter glue and stickers to decorate your Palace Ornament.
- At home, hang your ornament in front of a window and watch it sparkle!

Enrichment Idea

Children glue another CD to back of ornament and decorate both sides.

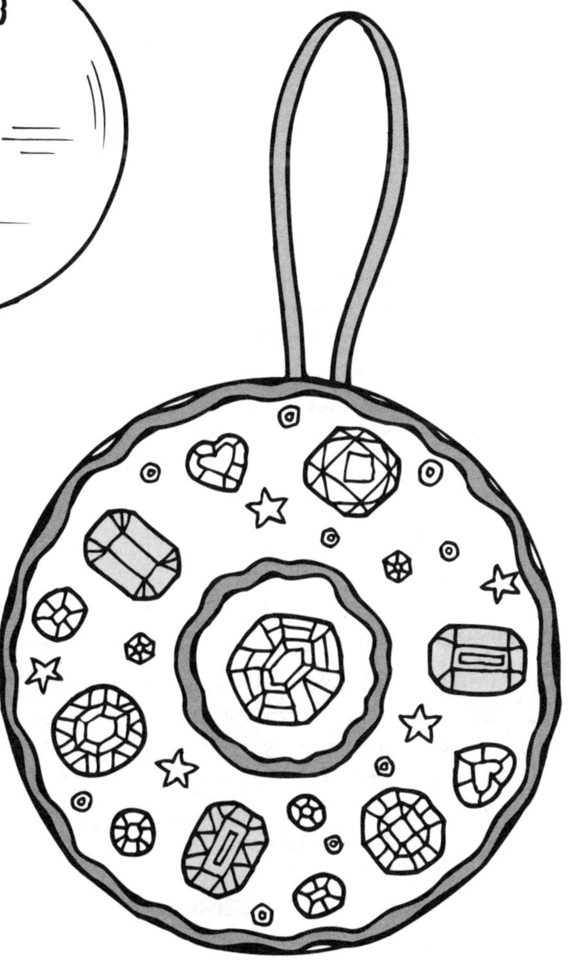

Morse Code Key Ring (25-30 MINUTES)

Materials

- Morse Code Alphabet (p. 55)
- drill with 3⁄16-inch (.5-cm) drill bit
- metal file
- fine-grit sandpaper
- acrylic craft paint in various colors
- card stock in various neon colors
- clear Con-Tact paper

For each child—

- 2- to 3-inch (5- to 7.7-cm) jar lid with pop-up top (applesauce, salsa, jelly)
- metal key ring

Standard Supplies

- shallow containers
- scissors
- ruler
- paintbrushes in various sizes
- hole punch

Preparation

Drill a hole in the side of the lid (sketch a). File off any sharp edges. Fold and tear sandpaper into small sections. Pour paint into shallow containers. Photocopy onto card stock one Morse Code Alphabet for each child. Cut Con-Tact paper into two 4x6-inch (10x15-cm) pieces for each child.

Conversation

When you train to do something, you must do it many times to learn how to do it properly. Training to use your Morse Code Key Ring will take practice. When you train to serve God you need to practice, too. What are some ways you can train to serve God, Alexis? (Read the Bible. Pray. Help others.)

Instruct each child in the following procedures:

- Use a section of sandpaper to sand the top, edges and sides of lids so there are no smooth spots and paint will adhere.
- Paint sanded surfaces with one color of paint. Set aside.
- Cut out Morse Code Alphabet card.
- With teacher's help, peel backing off one piece of clear Con-Tact paper. Place card in center of sticky side of Con-Tact paper and press (sketch b).
- Peel second piece of Con-Tact paper and stick it to the other side of the card so that both sides are covered. Press edges together.
- Trim edges of Con-Tact paper around card.
- Punch a hole in the card at the *X*.
- Thread the metal key ring through the hole in the card.
- Use small paintbrush to add dots, swirls, stripes or wiggles to painted lid. Let dry.
- With teacher's help, thread key ring through hole in lid.
- Press the center of the lid with your thumb to make a clicking sound.
- Use the Morse code card to practice clicking code words. Press and release quickly for a dot, slowly for a dash. Start with short, simple words, or practice the alphabet.

Simplification Idea

Before class, cut and cover cards with Con-Tact paper for children.

Budget Tip

Instead of using a key ring, tie a loop with elastic cord through card and lid. Make loop large enough to fit around a child's wrist.

a.

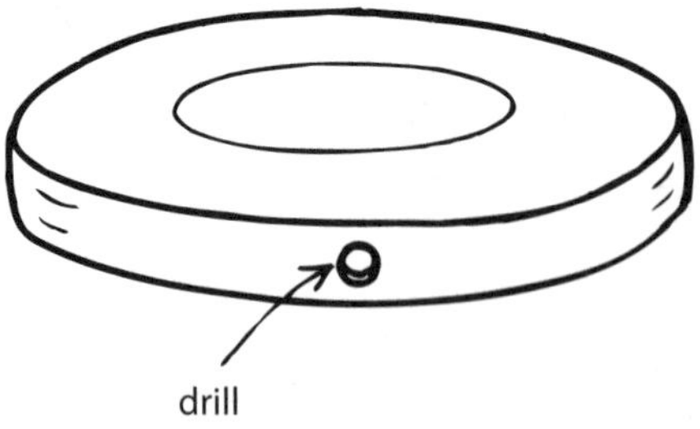

b.

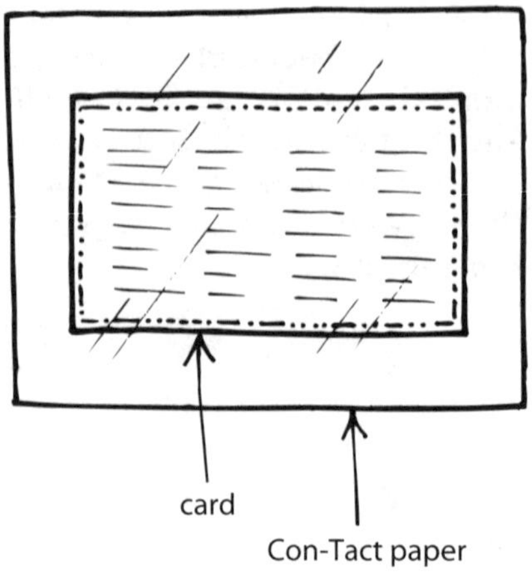

(X) Morse Code Alphabet

A •—	H ••••	N —•	T —
B —•••	I ••	O ———	U ••—
C —•—•	J •———	P •——•	V •••—
D —••	K —•—	Q ——•—	W •——
E •	L •—••	R •—•	X —••—
F ••—•	M ——	S •••	Y —•——
G ——•			Z ——••

(X) Morse Code Alphabet

A •—	H ••••	N —•	T —
B —•••	I ••	O ———	U ••—
C —•—•	J •———	P •——•	V •••—
D —••	K —•—	Q ——•—	W •——
E •	L •—••	R •—•	X —••—
F ••—•	M ——	S •••	Y —•——
G ——•			Z ——••

(X) Morse Code Alphabet

A •—	H ••••	N —•	T —
B —•••	I ••	O ———	U ••—
C —•—•	J •———	P •——•	V •••—
D —••	K —•—	Q ——•—	W •——
E •	L •—••	R •—•	X —••—
F ••—•	M ——	S •••	Y —•——
G ——•			Z ——••

(X) Morse Code Alphabet

A •—	H ••••	N —•	T —
B —•••	I ••	O ———	U ••—
C —•—•	J •———	P •——•	V •••—
D —••	K —•—	Q ——•—	W •——
E •	L •—••	R •—•	X —••—
F ••—•	M ——	S •••	Y —•——
G ——•			Z ——••

Planet Pictures (25-30 MINUTES)

Materials

- Planet Patterns (p. 57)
- Frame Back Pattern (p. 58)
- craft foam in various colors
- permanent marker
- poster board
- yarn
- one or two large plastic cones (available at sporting-goods stores)

For each child—

- 4-foot (1.2-m) length 18-gauge steel wire (available at hardware stores)

Standard Supplies

- scissors
- ruler
- hole punches
- craft glue

Preparation

Trace one set of Planet Patterns onto craft foam sheets for each child—each planet on a different color. Use permanent marker to mark dots at the top of each planet. Trace onto poster board three Frame Back Patterns for each child. Cut yarn into one 12-inch (30.5-cm) length for each child.

Conversation

Whose pictures will you put in your frame, Robert? Putting your mom's picture in your frame is a way to show love and honor to her. What is another way that you can honor your mom? The Bible says, *Be devoted to one another in brotherly love. Honor one another above yourselves* (Romans 12:10). **When you honor someone, you are making what he or she wants more important than what you want. When you clean your room without complaining, you are honoring your mom.**

Instruct each child in the following procedures:

- Choose and cut out one set of Planet Patterns, including the oval inside of each shape. Save foam scraps.
- Punch two holes at the top of each planet as indicated by the dots.
- Cut three frame backs from poster board.
- Squeeze a line of glue along curved edge of one frame back. Leave top edge free of glue, so that pictures can be inserted (sketch a). Press frame back onto back of one planet so that flat, unglued edge is at the top (sketch b). Repeat for other planets.
- Cut and punch foam scraps into strips, squiggles, dots, etc. Glue shapes onto planets to decorate. Let dry.
- Wrap wire around cone to make a spiral (sketch c). Carefully remove from cone, keeping spiral shape.
- Hold spiral so that wide end is at the top. Bend the end of wire at the top of spiral to make a loop for hanging. Tie a length of yarn onto loop (sketch c).
- Starting at the bottom of spiral, thread planets onto wire through punched holes. Space planets so they hang from different areas on the spiral. Beneath each planet, bend wire up slightly to stop planets from sliding off wire.
- At home, insert a picture into each planet. Hang Planet Picture Frame from a light fixture or ceiling.

Simplification Idea

Pre-cut Planet Patterns and Frame Back Patterns from foam and poster board.

Enrichment Idea

One or two days before craft, use a digital camera to photograph and print individual or group photos of children in front of a space backdrop. (Note: If your church has made the SonForce Kids VBS Mission Command Backdrop, photograph children in front of Mission Command.) Children insert photos into completed frames.

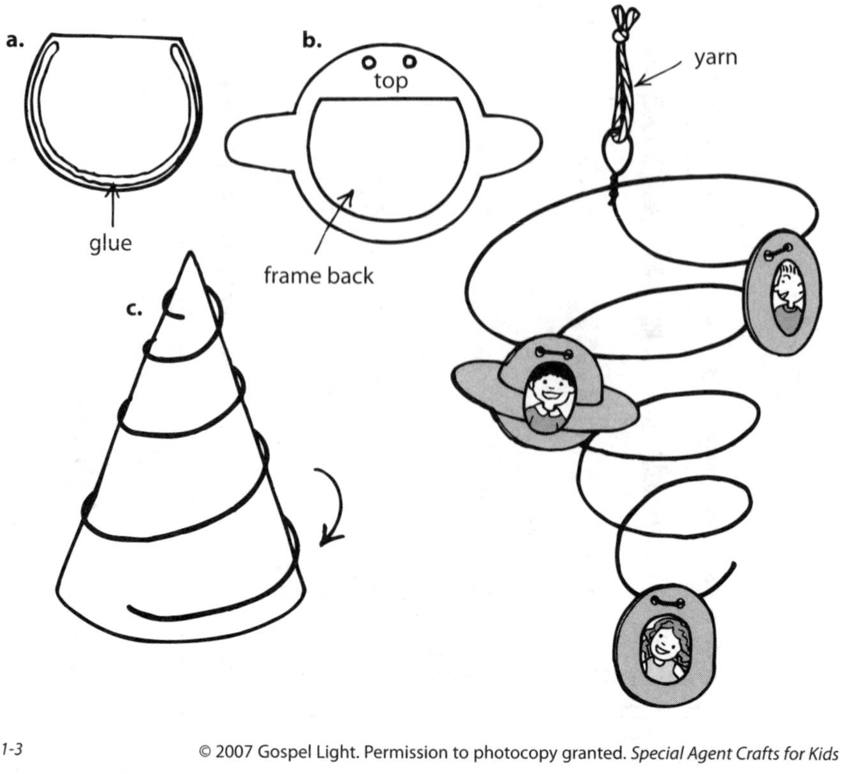

Planet Patterns

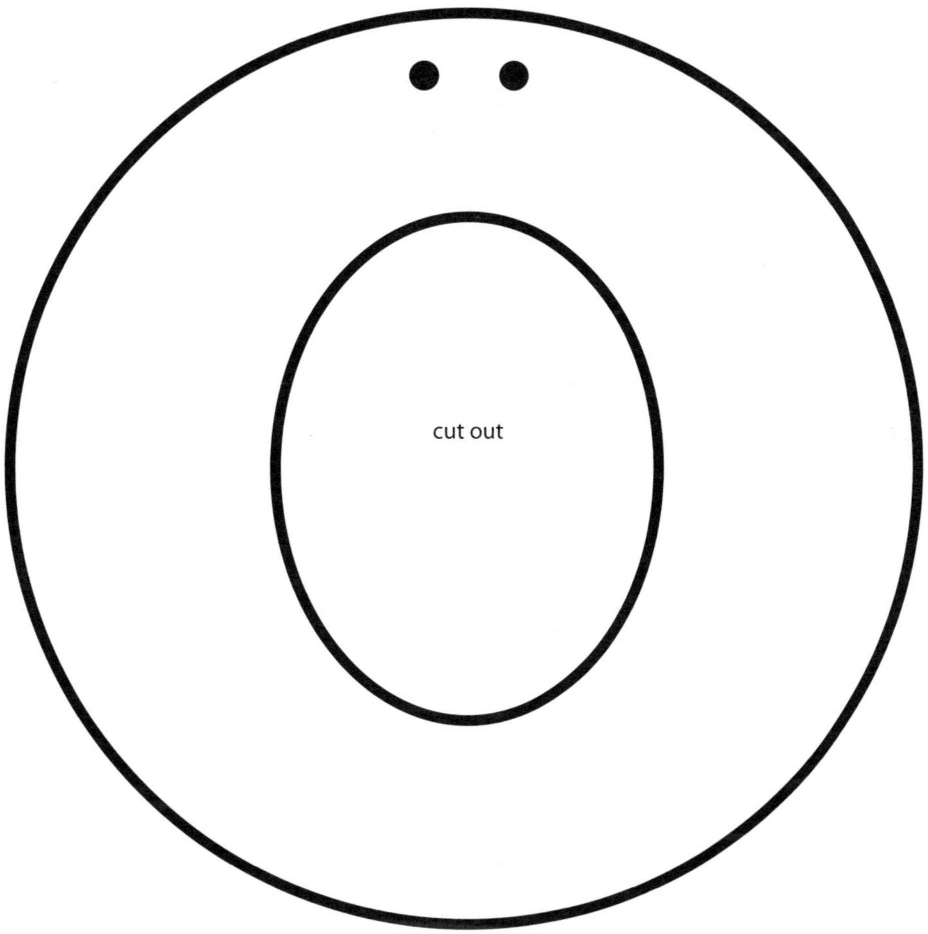

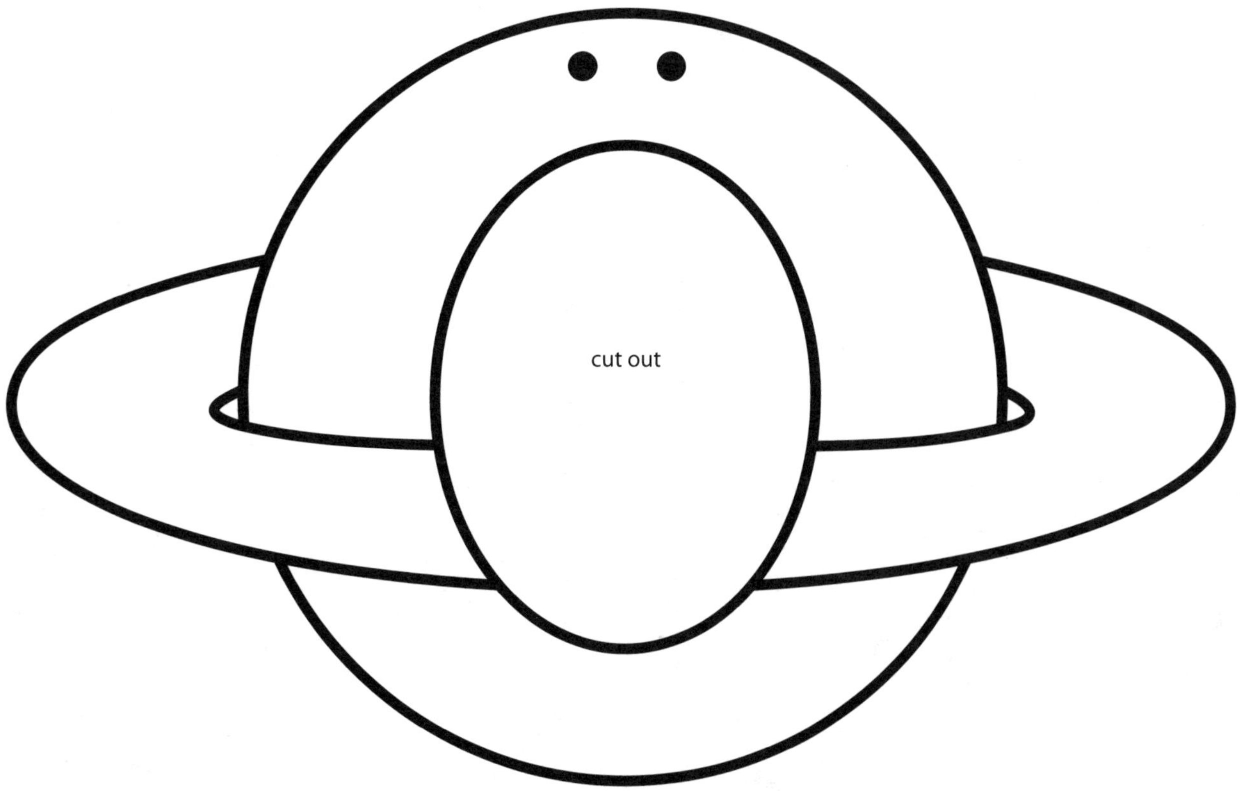

Planet Patterns, cont.

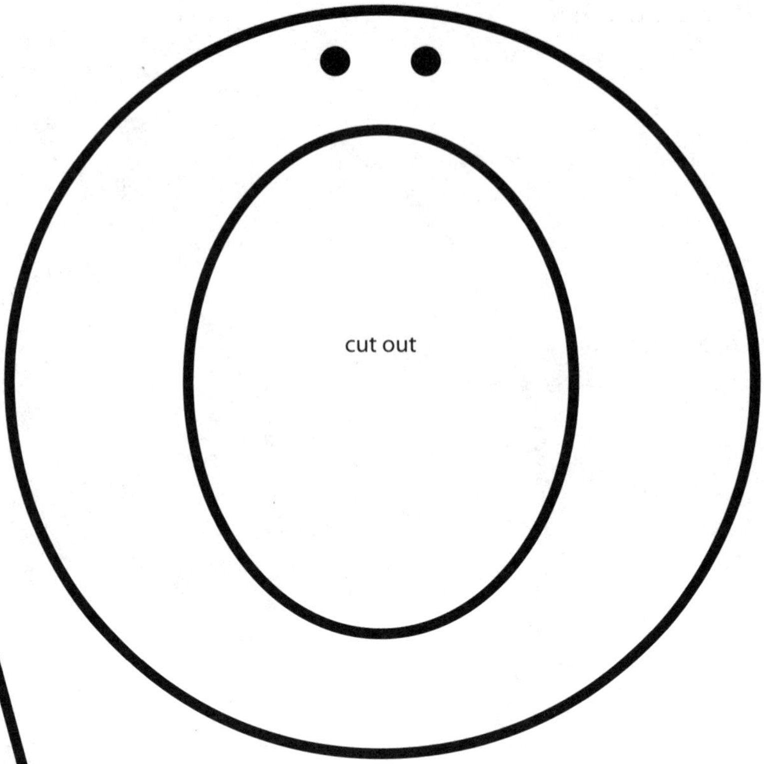

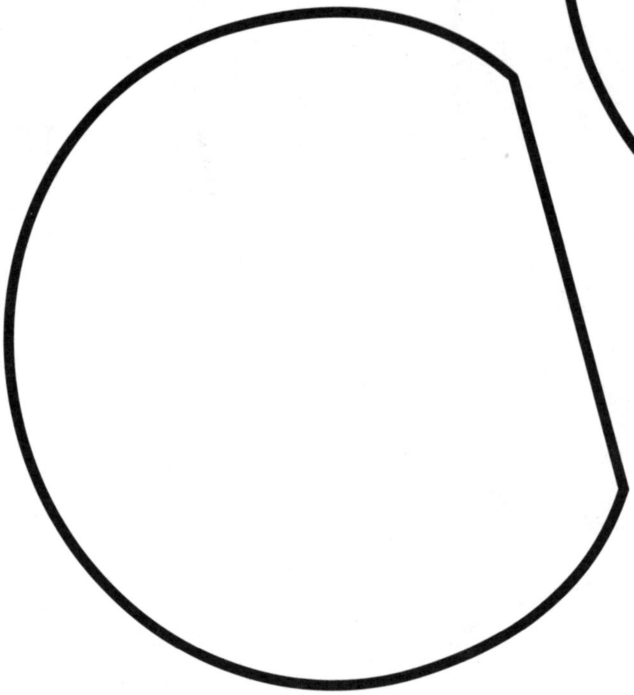

Frame Back Pattern

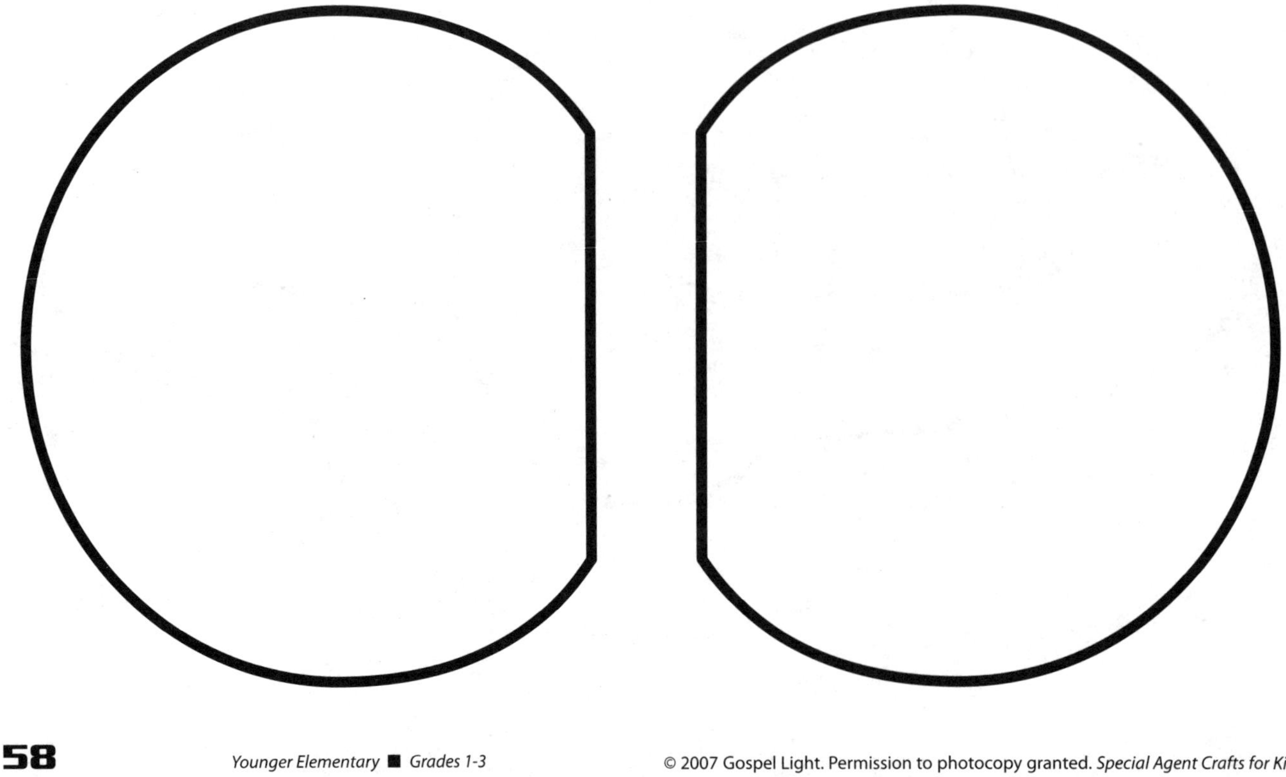

SFA Message Carrier (20-25 MINUTES)

Materials

- black poster board
- gold or silver embroidery floss
- electrical tape in neon colors
- gel pens
- brightly colored stickers in geometric shapes

For each child—

- four 3½x6½-inch (9x16.5-cm) standard-sized envelopes
- 1-inch (2.5-cm) diameter button with shank

Standard Supplies

- scissors
- measuring stick
- hole punch

Preparation

Cut poster board into one 6½x11-inch (16.5x28-cm) rectangle for each child. Cut floss into one 44-inch (112-cm) length for each child. Fold poster board as shown in sketch a. Cut four 6½-inch (16.5-cm) lengths of electrical tape for each child. (Hint: Stick tape pieces around a table or counter so that children can easily remove them when needed.)

Conversation

What messages will you put inside your Message Carrier? You can give messages to your friends, too. Queen Esther sent messages to her people through Mordecai. The Bible says, *Be devoted to one another in brotherly love. Honor one another above yourselves* (Romans 12:10)**. What does it mean to show brotherly love?** (Caring for others as we would for someone in our own family.) **Who is someone you can show brotherly love to here at VBS?**

Instruct each child in the following procedures:

- Open poster board. Place one envelope along fold line (sketch b).
- Tape bottom of envelope to poster board along fold line as shown in sketch b. (Make sure the flap of envelope does not get taped down.)
- Repeat process with other three envelopes, taping each one on top of the one before it.
- Punch hole in poster board (sketch c).
- Thread floss through shank of button. Pull floss through button until button is in the middle of floss (sketch d). Insert both ends of floss through punched hole and pull until button is stopped by hole (sketch d).
- To close Message Carrier, wrap doubled floss around back of carrier and pull to the front. Wind floss around button to secure (sketch e).
- Decorate Message Carrier with gel pens and stickers.

Enrichment Idea

Children draw pictures and write messages to stick inside envelopes of their Message Carriers or to give to others.

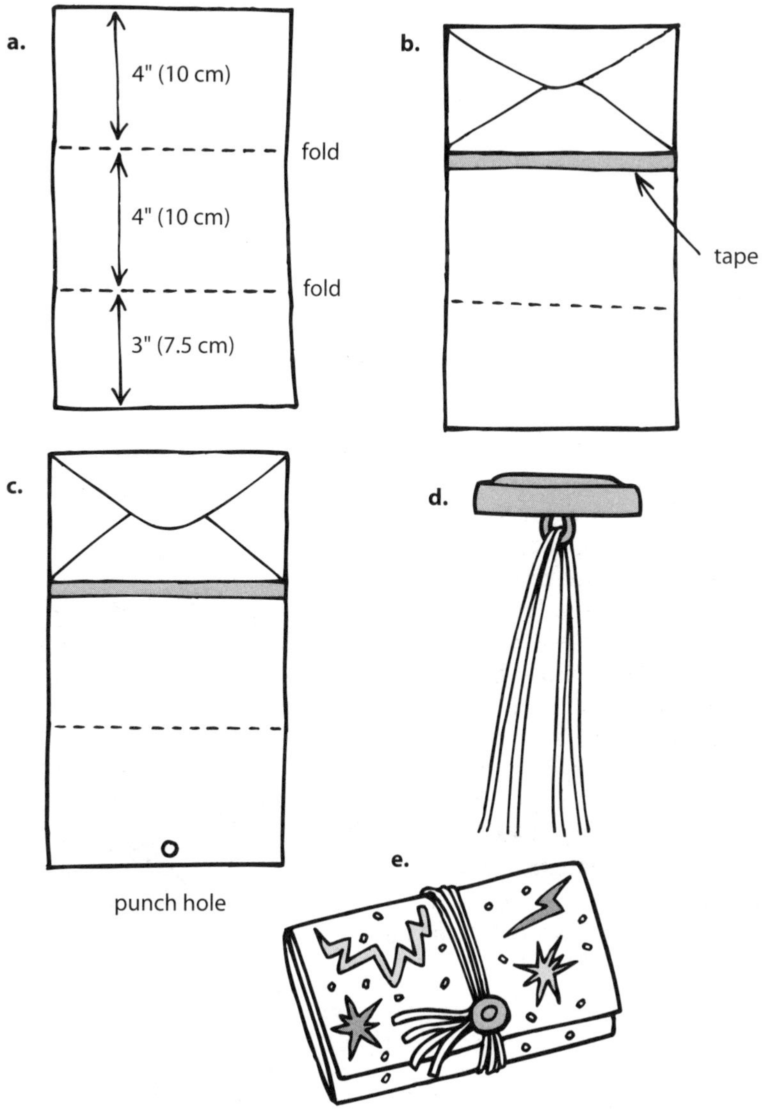

Jeremiah's Message (20-25 MINUTES)

Materials

- Old Hebrew Letters (p. 61)
- jute
- black tempera paint

For each child—

- brown paper grocery bag

Standard Supplies

- newspaper
- scissors
- measuring stick
- shallow containers
- scrap paper
- thin-tipped paintbrushes

Preparation

Cover work area with newspaper. Cut jute into one 12-inch (30.5-cm) length for each child. Cut bags into one 18x12-inch (45.5x30.5-cm) rectangle for each child. Photocopy one Old Hebrew Letters page for every two children and cut apart. Pour paint into shallow containers.

Conversation

The Bible tells us that God told Jeremiah and Baruch to write down God's messages on a scroll and then tell them to the people. But when the king heard, he destroyed Jeremiah's scroll! Jeremiah and Baruch had the courage to do what God wanted and write another scroll, even though they knew the king would be mad! Jeremiah 7:23 says, *Walk in all the ways I command you, that it may go well with you.* What is a way that you can obey God? (Tell the truth. Invite a new kid to play. Be kind, even when someone has been mean.)

Instruct each child in the following procedures:

- Crumple paper rectangle into a tight ball, and then smooth it out again (sketch a). Repeat several times to give rectangle the look of ancient paper.
- Using Old Hebrew Letters sheet as an example, paint several old Hebrew letters or write the ancient Hebrew word for God onto paper (sketch b). (Hint: Practice painting letters on scrap paper before painting on your scroll.) Let dry.
- Roll up paper to form a scroll, and then tie closed with jute (sketch c).
- Make additional scrolls as time and interest allow.

Simplification Idea

Instead of paint, children use black fine-tip permanent markers to write letters.

Enrichment Ideas

Children glue a wooden dowel to each short edge of scroll. They roll up and tie scrolls closed using leather lacing.

a.

b.

c.

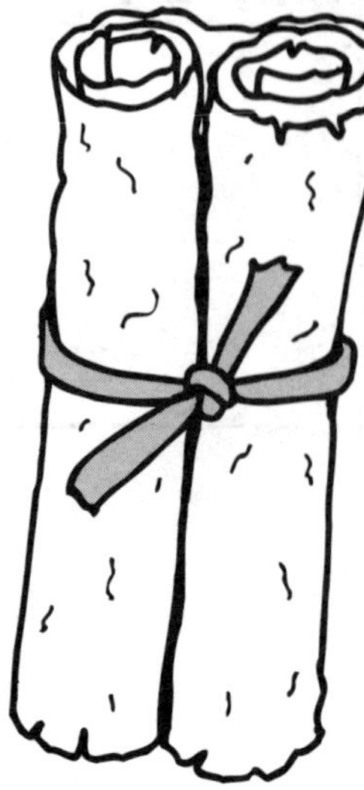

Old Hebrew Letters

These are some of the Hebrew letters that Baruch would have used when writing the scroll.

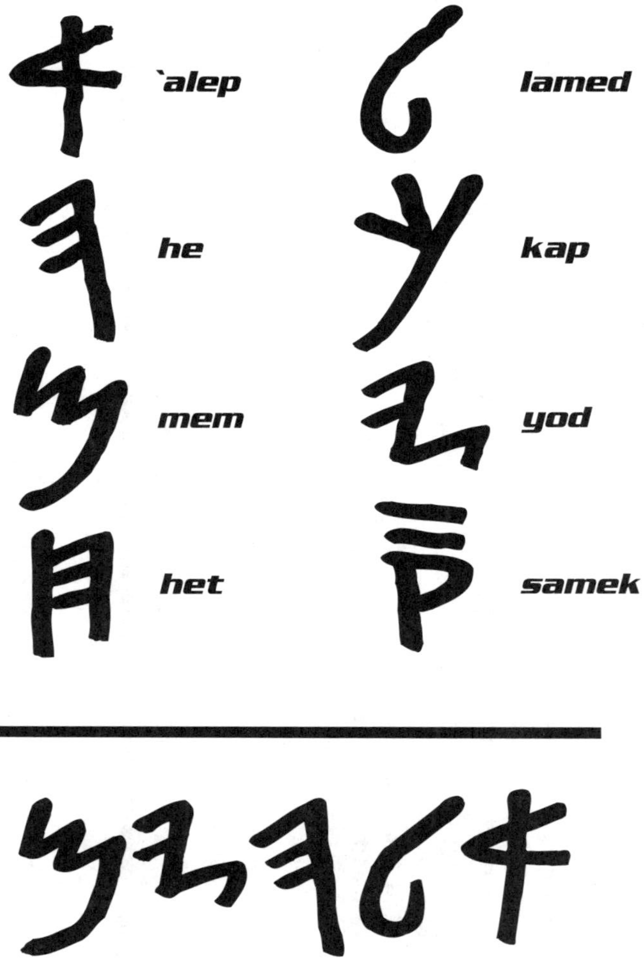

God (Elohim)

Old Hebrew Letters

These are some of the Hebrew letters that Baruch would have used when writing the scroll.

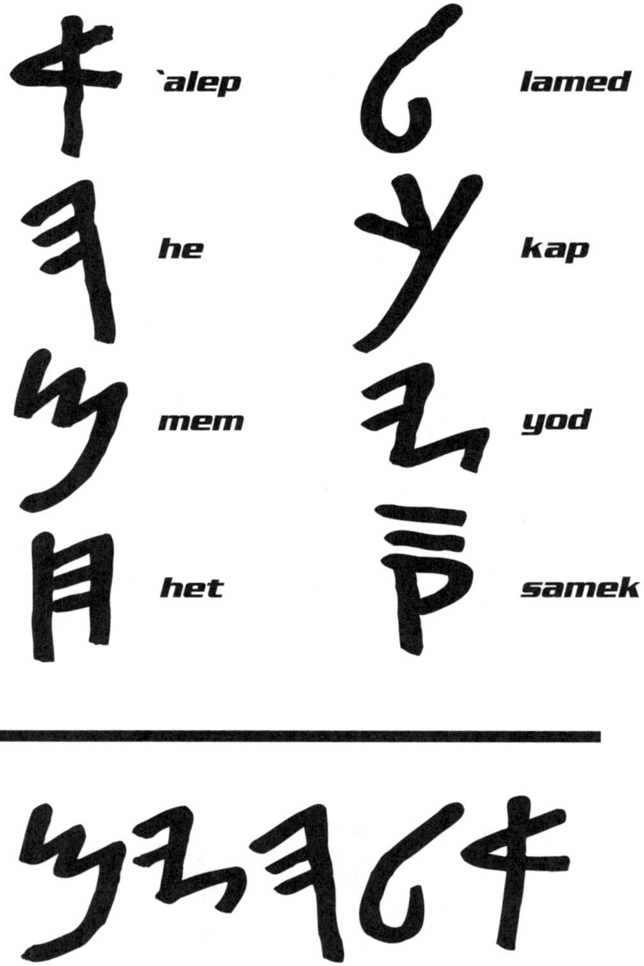

God (Elohim)

Daily Mission Log (25-30 MINUTES)

Materials

- Hinge Pattern (p. 62)
- craft foam sheets in various colors

For each child—

- two discarded CDs
- two paper fasteners
- 3-inch (7.5-cm) square Post-it pad

Standard Supplies

- pen
- scissors
- craft glue

Preparation

Trace Hinge Pattern onto craft foam sheet, making one for each child. Mark dots where indicated.

Conversation

What do you think it means to "follow in God's path"? (To obey God. To do the good and right things that He wants you to do.) **Before you can follow in God's path, first you need to know what He wants you to do! One way to know more about God's path is to read His Word, the Bible. You can write verses or promises from the Bible in your Logbook to help you remember them.**

Instruct each child in the following procedures:

- Trace a CD onto craft foam and cut out to make two foam circles. Glue one foam circle onto the label side of each CD.
- Cut out Hinge Pattern.
- Poke one fastener through each dot on the Hinge Pattern (sketch a).
- Poke one fastener through the center of one foam-backed CD (sketch b). On foam side, open fastener (sketch c). Repeat with second fastener and second CD, fastening CD to other end of Hinge Pattern.
- Peel back off Post-it pad and glue pad onto foam side of one CD (sketch d).
- Fold Logbook closed.

Enrichment Idea

Use permanent markers to draw designs or write a title or name on CD covering logbook. Cut shapes from foam scraps and glue to the cover of logbook.

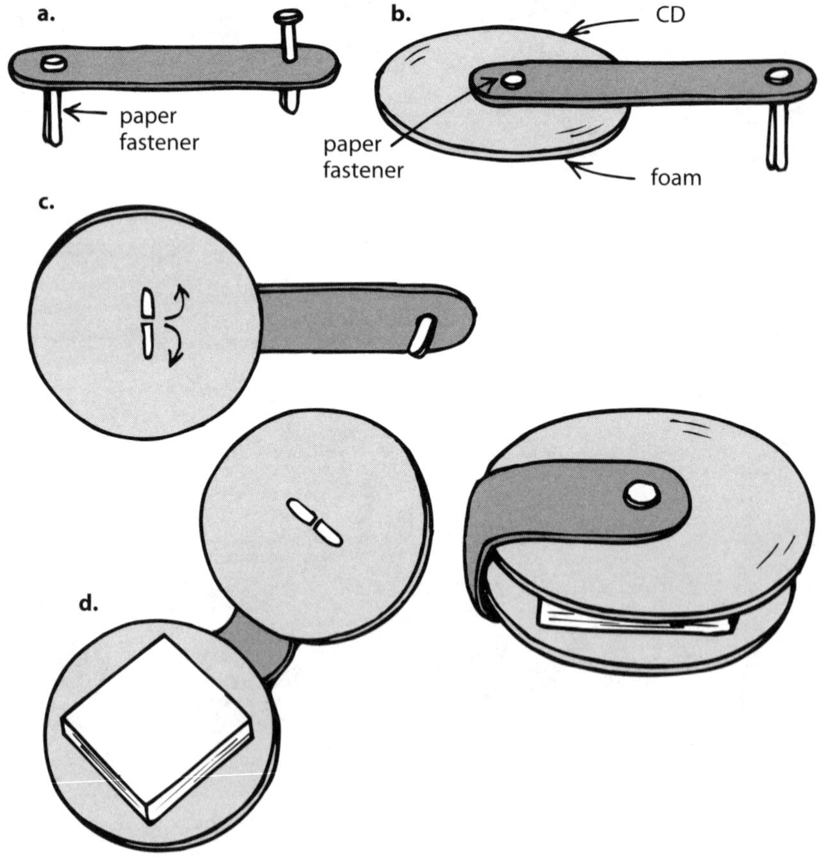

Hinge Pattern

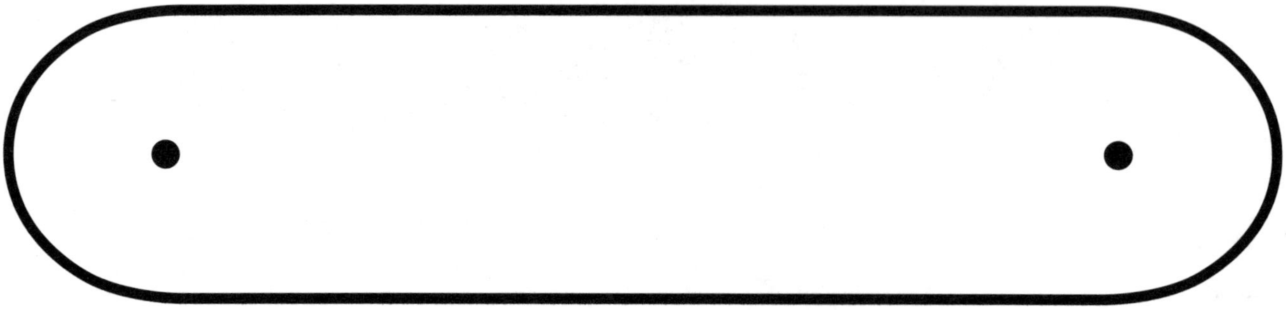

SFA Promise Viewer (25-30 MINUTES)

Materials

- Promise Pattern (p. 64)
- Viewer Pattern (p. 65)
- poster board in a metallic or neon color
- star or space stickers
- metallic gel pens or colored markers
- black fine-tip permanent markers

For each child—

- paper-towel tube

Optional—

- Daily Missions and SonForce Assortment stickers (available from Gospel Light)

Standard Supplies

- card stock
- craft knife
- scissors
- glue sticks
- transparent tape

Preparation

Photocopy one Promise Pattern onto card stock for each child. Trace one Viewer Pattern onto poster board for each child; use craft knife to cut out the two windows in each pattern, and then cut out all Viewer Patterns.

Conversation

Your Promise Viewer will help you remember some of God's promises. Which one is your favorite promise, Annie? Remembering God's promises can help us to have courage in all situations. The Bible says, *Be strong and courageous . . . for the Lord your God will be with you wherever you go* (Joshua 1:9). God loves you. You can believe all of the promises in His Word.

Instruct each child in the following procedures:

- Cut out Promise Pattern.
- Wrap the Promise Pattern around the paper-towel tube and glue onto tube (sketch a).
- Completely cover the long edge of the Promise Pattern with transparent tape (sketch b).
- Decorate Viewer Pattern with stickers and pens or markers.
- Wrap Viewer Pattern around tube so that the longer window lines up with the words to the Bible verses and the shorter window lines up with the verse's reference (sketch c). The edges of poster board will overlap. Viewer should be snug, but not tight. Secure overlapping edge with transparent tape (sketch c). (Hint: Pair up with a friend to help hold and tape each other's Viewers.)
- Twist the tube to reveal God's promises and their matching references in the windows.

Simplification Idea

Before class, cut out and glue Promise Pattern to tubes for children.

a.

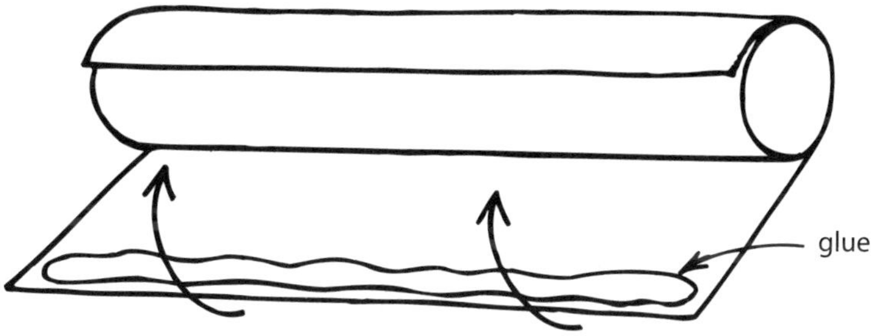

b.

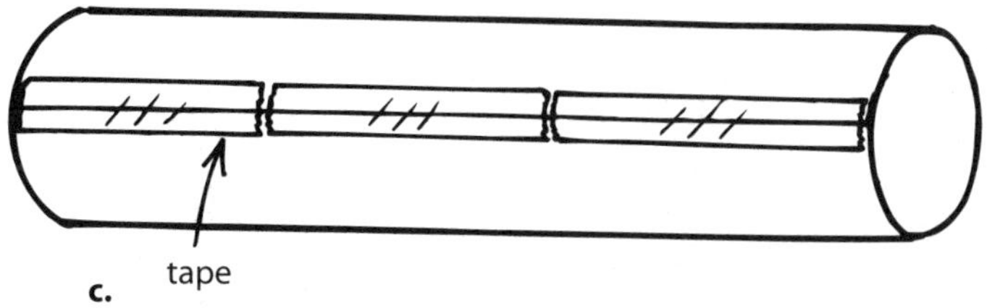

c.

Promise Pattern

cut

Jeremiah 17:7

Romans 12:10

Proverbs 19:20

Jeremiah 7:23

Joshua 1:9

"Blessed is the man who trusts in the Lord, whose confidence is in him."

"Be devoted to one another in brotherly love. Honor one another above yourselves."

"Listen to advice and accept instruction, and in the end you will be wise."

"Walk in all the ways I command you, that it may go well with you."

"Be strong and courageous . . . for the Lord your God will be with you wherever you go."

cut

Viewer Pattern

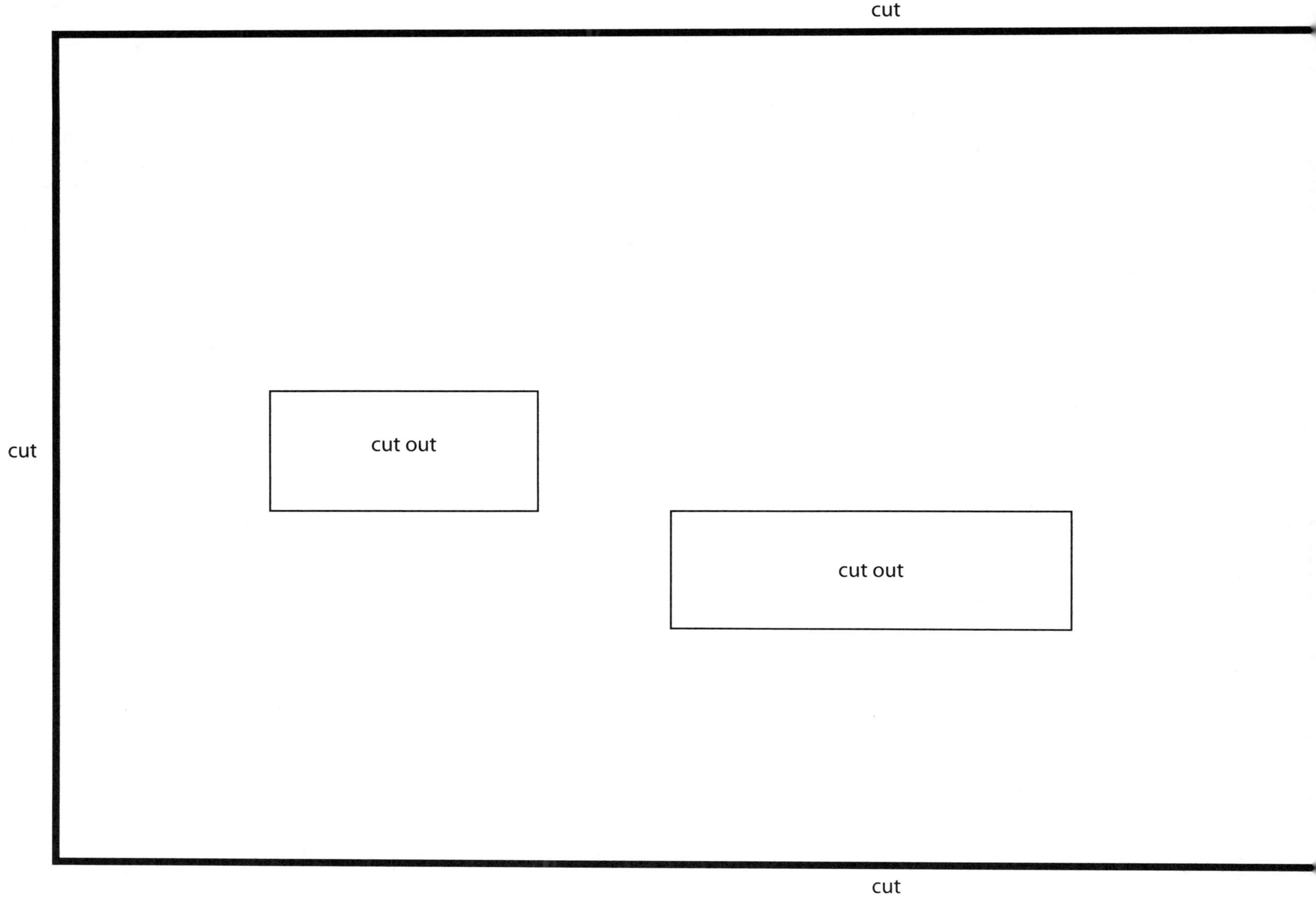

Moses Marble Maze

(TWO-DAY CRAFT/35-45 MINUTES TOTAL TIME)

Materials

- Maze Pattern (p. 68)
- Egyptian Palace Pattern (p. 67)
- Hebrew Home Pattern (p. 67)
- metallic blue spray-paint
- corkscrew pasta

For each child—

- shallow box at least 8½x11 inches (21.5x28 cm) across the bottom (pizza box, cardboard tray from a case of water bottles or a taller box cut down to approximately 2 inches [5 cm] high)
- marble

Standard Supplies

- card stock
- newspaper
- crayons or markers
- craft glue
- scissors
- transparent tape

Conversation

The King of Egypt wanted to hurt baby Moses and other Hebrew babies. But God had important plans for Moses, so He protected Moses. Who did God use to keep baby Moses safe? (His family. Pharaoh's daughter.) **God has special plans for each of us, too. We can trust God's plans for us, even when we are in a difficult situation. Jeremiah 17:7 says, *Blessed is the man who trusts in the Lord, whose confidence is in him.***

DAY ONE

Preparation

Photocopy onto card stock one Maze, one Egyptian Palace and one Hebrew Home Pattern for each child. Cover outdoor work area with newspaper. Spray-paint pasta. (Hint: To thoroughly cover pasta with paint, use an old wooden spoon and stir pasta around on paper as you paint.) Let pasta dry.

Instruct each child in the following procedures:

- Color Maze Pattern.
- Glue maze to inside bottom of the box.
- Glue pasta along the heavy lines of your maze. Let dry.

DAY TWO

Instruct each child in the following procedures:

- Color Egyptian Palace and Hebrew Home Patterns.
- Cut out patterns along heavy lines, fold along dashed lines and tape as shown in sketch a.
- Glue Egyptian Palace facing the "Start" of your maze. Glue Hebrew Home facing the "Finish" of your maze (sketch b). Let glue dry.
- Place marble inside Egyptian Palace. Roll marble out the door, along the maze and into the Hebrew Home.

Enrichment Idea

Children glue small stones, sand, and/or plastic trees and animals around the maze for an added 3-D effect.

a.

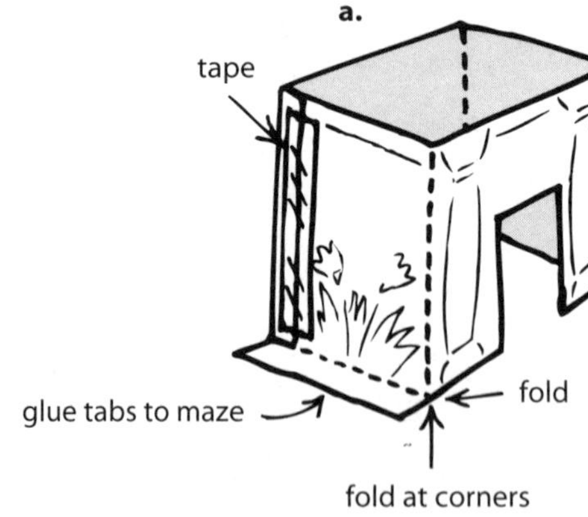

b.

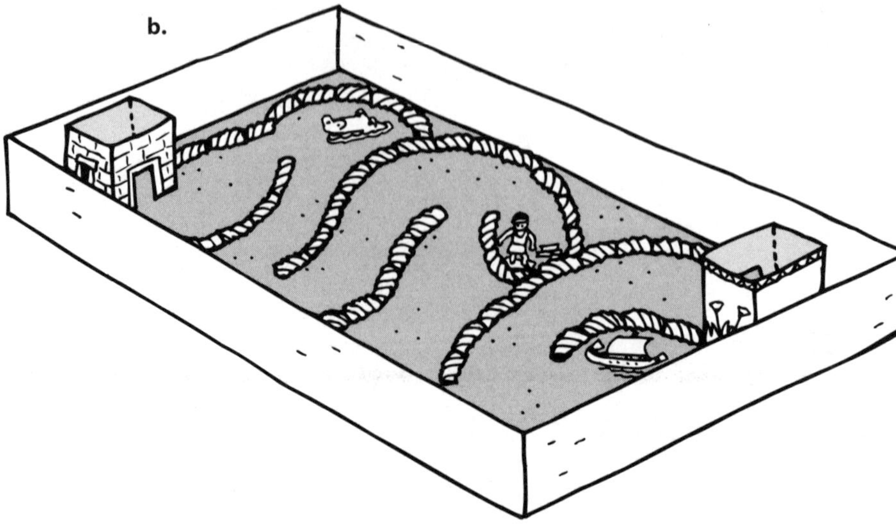

Egyptian Palace Pattern

Hebrew Home Pattern

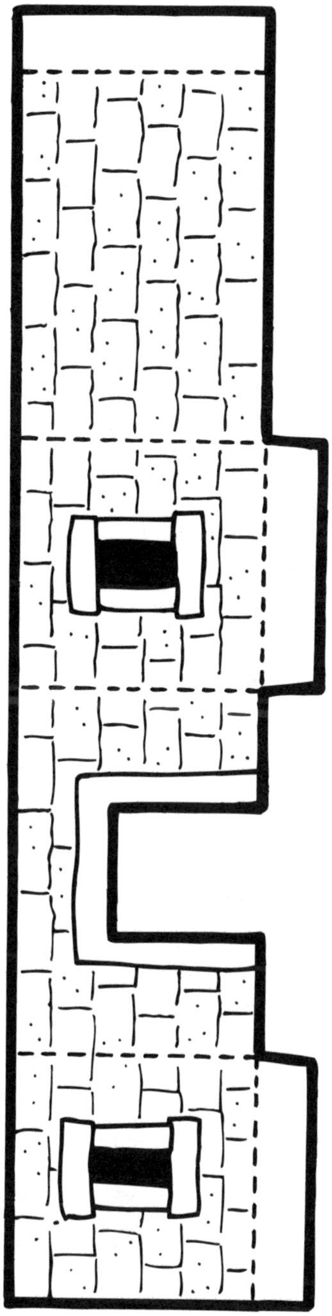

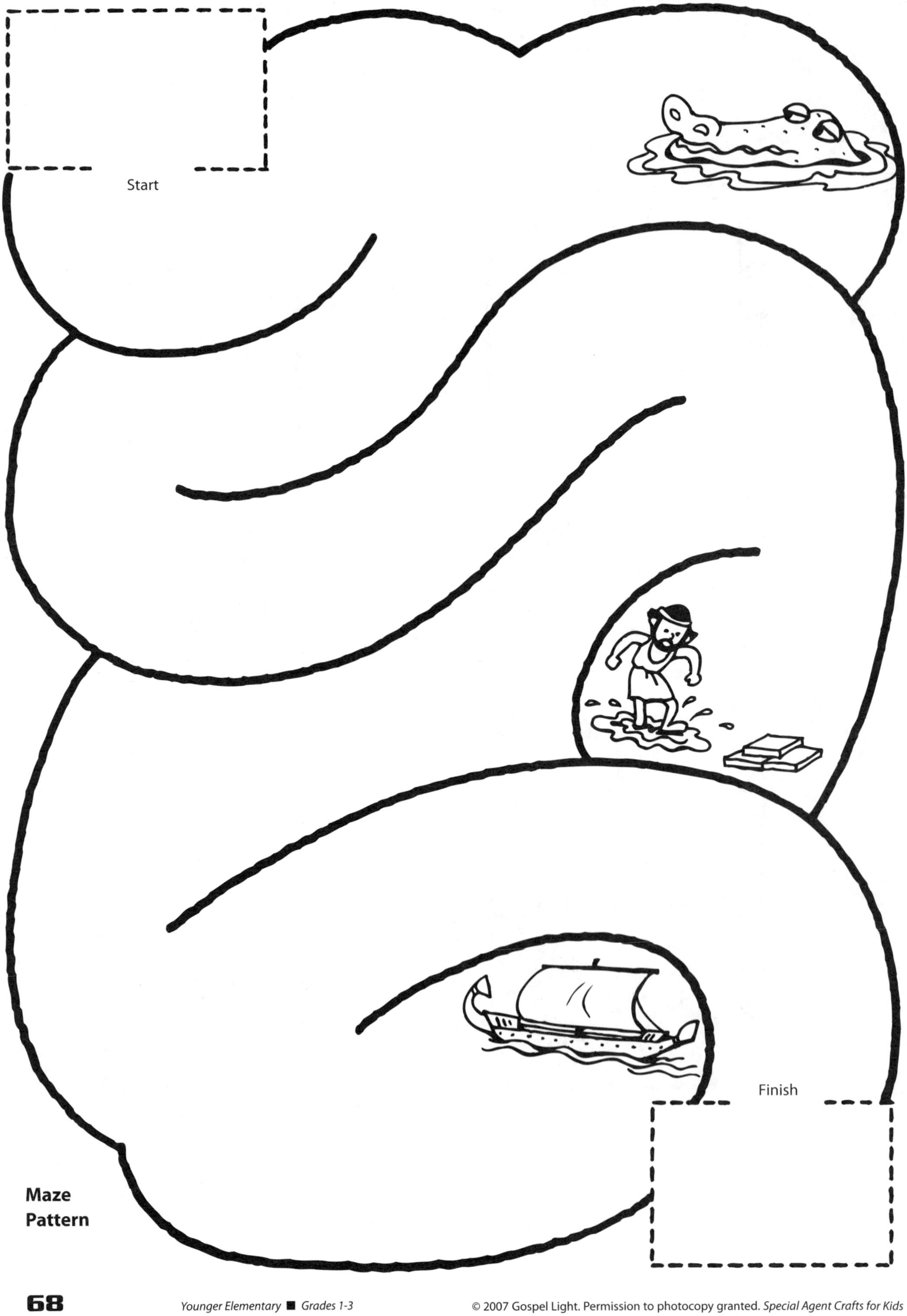

Maze Pattern

SECTION THREE

Grades 4-6

Crafts for Older Elementary

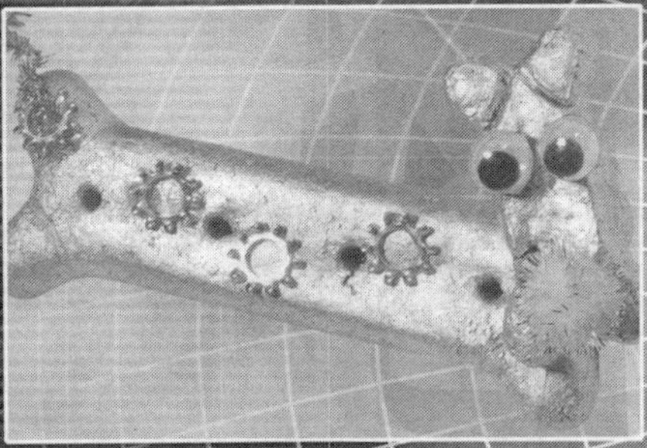

Planning craft projects for older children can be fun. These children have well-developed skills to complete more complicated projects and they love the chance to use those skills. However, preteens also have well-developed preferences about what they want to do. Sometimes a challenging project may not appeal to these young sophisticates, while a project that seems too juvenile to the adult will click with the kids!

We think you'll find projects in this section to satisfy the varied tastes of older elementary children. But a sense of humor and these tips will surely help: Filter craft ideas through a panel of experts—two or three fifth graders! If they like something, chances are the rest of the group will, too. Also, the better you get to know your children, the better your batting average will be. Remember, kids enjoy adapting crafts to express their own personalities—so put out a few extra supplies such as wiggle eyes, glitter glue, and fabric or paper scraps. You just might be surprised at what they dream up!

SonForce Mouse Pad (15-20 MINUTES)

Materials

- acrylic paint in various neon colors
- clear Con-Tact paper
- stickers with space themes
- fine-tip permanent markers

For each child—

- 9x12-inch (23x30.5-cm) sheet of craft foam

Standard Supplies

- scissors
- measuring stick
- shallow containers
- craft glue
- thin-tipped paintbrushes

Preparation

Cut craft foam sheets in half to make two 6x9-inch (15x23-cm) rectangles for each child. Pour paint into shallow containers. Cut Con-Tact paper into one 8x11-inch (20.5x28-cm) rectangle for each child.

Conversation

Computers contain millions of pieces of information that can be useful when you need to know about something. They are helpful tools. Where can you find information when you need to know about God? (The Bible. Church.) **The Bible says, *Obey me, and I will be your God and you will be my people. Walk in all the ways I command you, that it may go well with you*** (Jeremiah 7:23)**. Our Bible teaches us about God's ways and His plans for us. Reading our Bibles will help us learn more about how to follow God.**

Instruct each child in the following procedures:

- Glue craft foam sheets back-to-back to make a thicker mouse pad.
- Use paint, stickers and markers to make designs on your mouse pad (sketch a). Let dry.
- Peel backing from Con-Tact paper and place sticky side up on table. Place mouse pad face down onto center of Con-Tact paper.
- Trim off all corners of Con-Tact paper and wrap edges over mouse pad (sketch b).

a.

b.

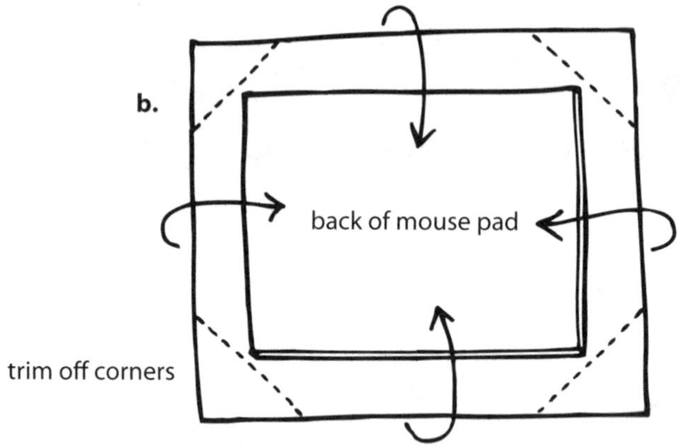

Galaxy Glow Tube (15-20 MINUTES)

Materials

- ¾-inch (1.9-cm) clear, vinyl tubing (available at hardware stores)
- low-temperature glue gun
- several pitchers
- star-shaped plastic confetti
- glitter
- small metallic-colored beads
- glow-in-the-dark pony beads
- several plastic bins
- blue food coloring
- funnels

For each child—

- two corks to fit ends of tubing

Standard Supplies

- craft knife
- measuring stick
- water
- disposable cups

Preparation

Use craft knife to cut tubing into one 18-inch (45.5-cm) length for each child. Plug in glue gun out of reach of children. Fill pitchers with water.

Conversation

How many stars do you think there are in the whole universe? Only God knows for sure! Would you like to be an astronaut, Julian? It takes a lot of courage to go into space, but God has made us a promise. In the Bible God says, ***Be strong and courageous. Do not be terrified; do not be discouraged, for the Lord your God will be with you wherever you go*** (Joshua 1:9)**. God has promised that no matter where we go, He will be with us. Because God always keeps His promises, we can believe it. And we can tell others about His promises, too!**

Instruct each child in the following procedures:

- With teacher's help, use glue gun to glue around the circumference of one cork. Quickly push cork into one end of tube to seal the end (sketch a). Allow glue to set for a minute or two.
- Place two or three pinches of confetti into tube. Add a pinch or two each of glitter and beads.
- Working over a plastic bin, pour water into a cup. Add a few drops of blue food coloring to cup. Use a funnel to pour water from the cup slowly into the tube (tube will fill quickly). Fill tube to within ½ inch (1.3 cm) from the top (sketch b).
- Hold tube upright. With teacher's help, use glue gun to apply glue around the second cork. Push cork into end of tube. Allow glue to set a minute or two to make sure glue seals tube end.
- Tip the tube back and forth to mix the food coloring with the water. Watch the stars glitter in space.

a.

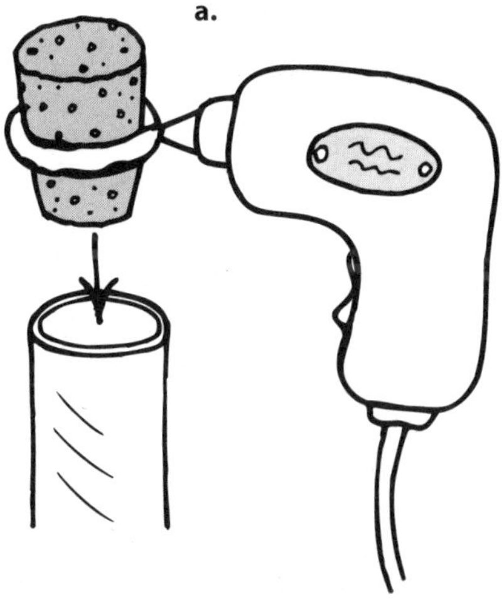

b.

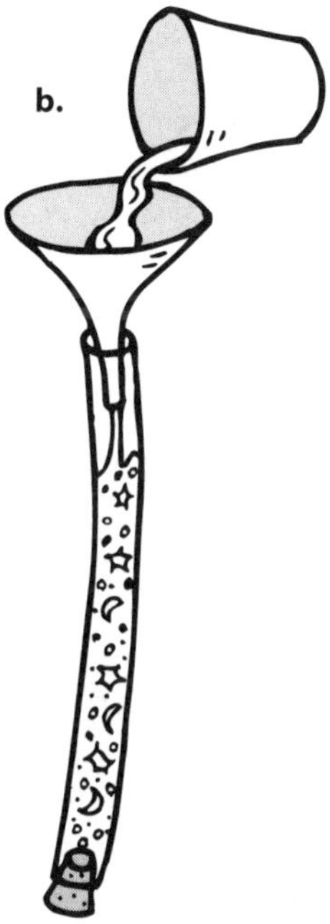

Constellation Clings *(15-20 MINUTES)*

Materials

- Constellation Patterns (p. 73)
- lightweight clear vinyl (available at fabric stores in the upholstery section)
- squeeze bottles of glow-in-the-dark and glitter paints
- fine-tip permanent markers in various colors

Standard Supplies

- scissors
- ruler

Preparation

Photocopy one set of Constellation Patterns for every three children; cut patterns apart to separate. Cut vinyl into one 9x12-inch (23x30.5-cm) rectangle for each child.

Instruct each child in the following procedures:

- Lay vinyl rectangle over a Constellation Pattern. Use permanent marker to trace constellation onto vinyl. Paint stars in constellations (sketch a).
- Repeat process with other Constellation Pattern. Let dry.
- Cut around painted constellations (sketch b).
- Vinyl constellations can be pressed onto a smooth, clean window.

Enrichment Idea

Use vinyl scraps to make additional clings by drawing and painting stars, comets and planets.

a.

b.

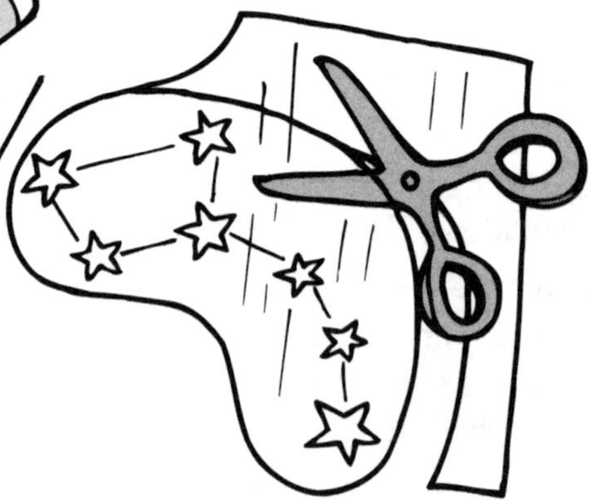

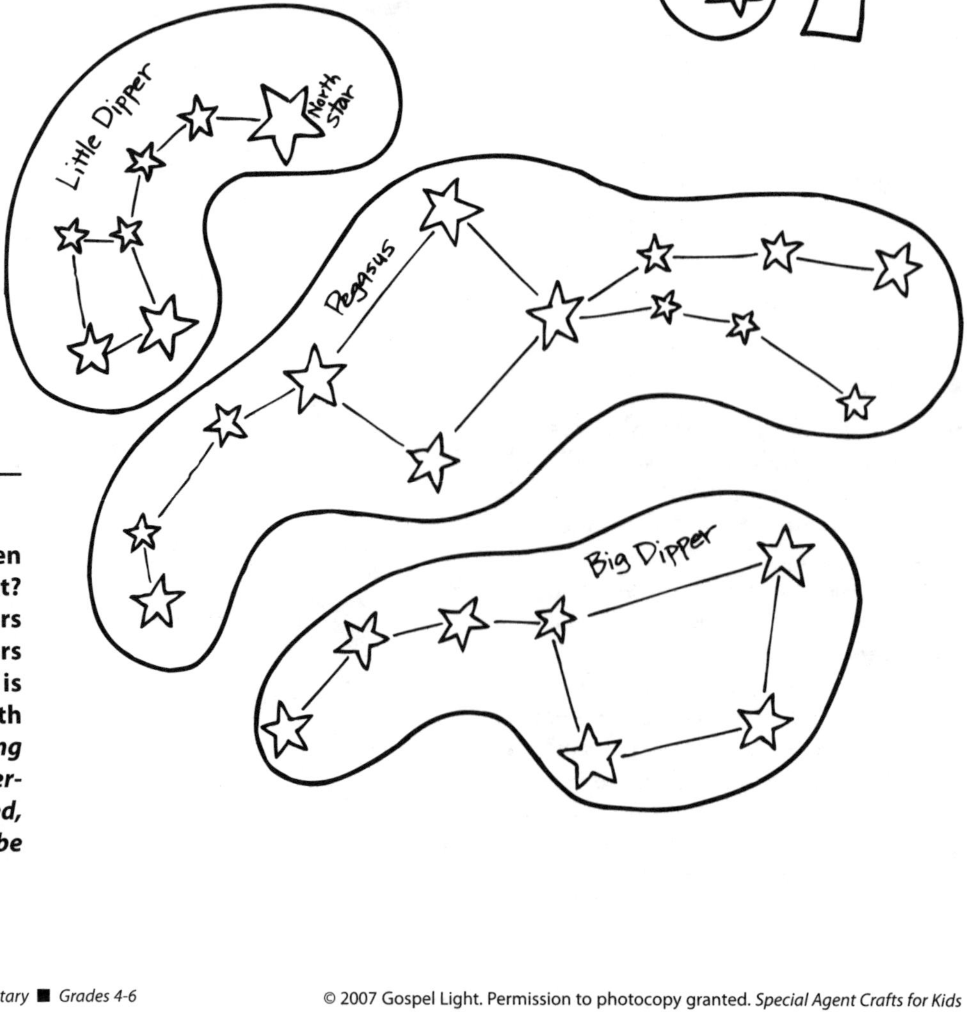

Conversation

What do you think about when you look at the stars at night? What do you think the stars tell us about God? The stars can remind you that God is powerful and is always with you. Joshua 1:9 says, *Be strong and courageous. Do not be terrified; do not be discouraged, for the Lord your God will be with you wherever you go.*

Constellation Patterns

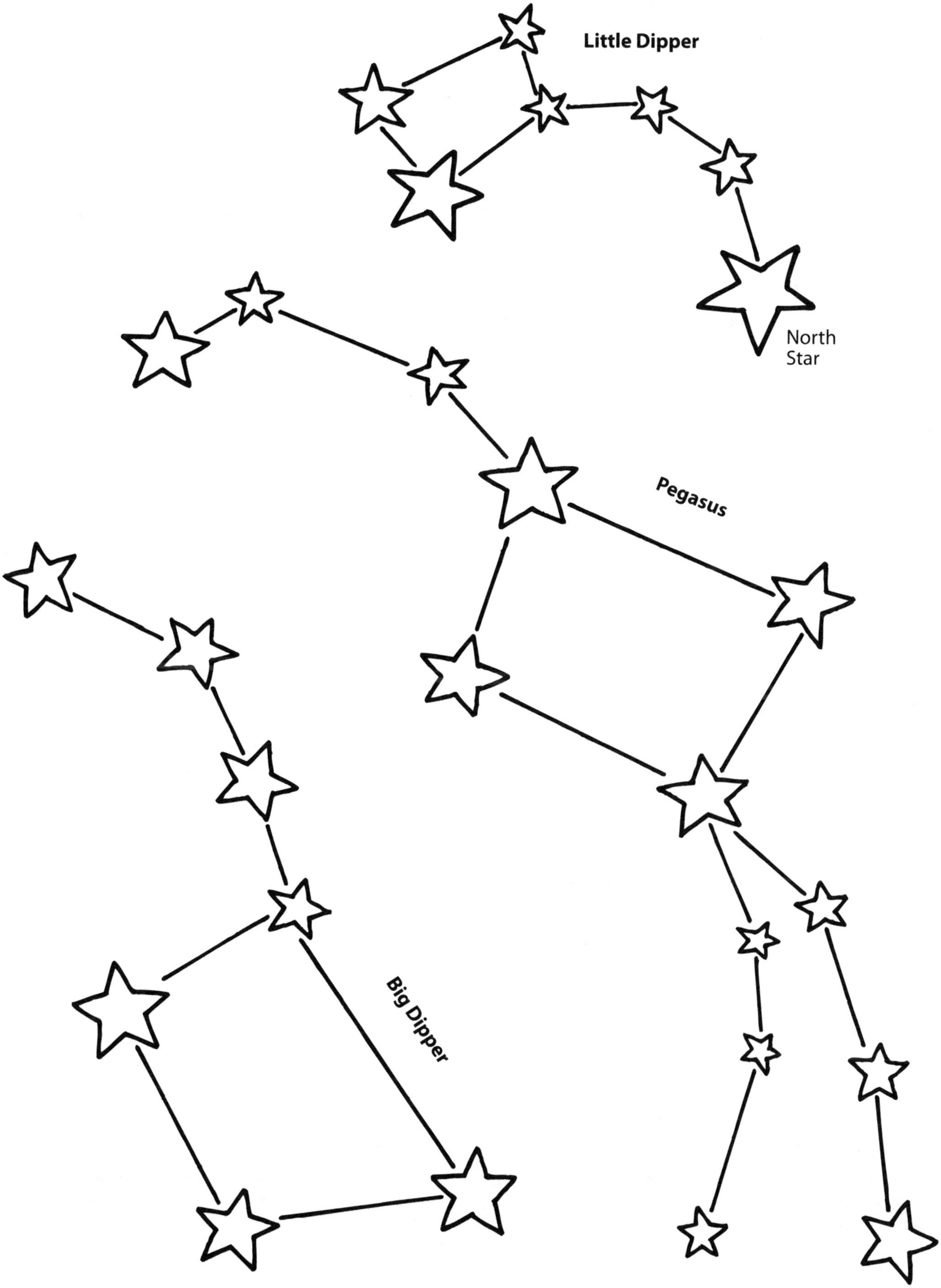

SonForce Agent Kit (20-25 MINUTES)

Materials

- SonForce Agent Kit Patterns (pp. 75-77)
- fabric paint in squeeze bottles
- permanent markers in various colors
- colored pencils

For each child—

- one zippered pencil holder with binder holes
- scissors

Standard Supplies

- card stock

Preparation

Photocopy onto card stock one set of SonForce Agent Kit Patterns for each child.

Instruct each child in the following procedures:

- Use paint and markers to add designs (dots, swirls, flowers, hearts, sunbursts, squiggles) to the front of your pencil holder. Let dry.
- Cut out and color SonForce Agent Kit Patterns and add to kit.

Simplification Idea

Use stickers instead of paint to create designs on bag.

Enrichment Idea

Children add other items to kits, such as adhesive bandages, small compass or flashlight, tissues, hand wipes and sunglasses.

Conversation

When special agents work they use many different types of tools. They follow a map so that they don't get lost. They study survival tips so that they will know what to do in difficult situations. What is something that a special agent for God uses to help him or her every day? (Bible.) **The Bible says, *Obey me, and I will be your God and you will be my people. Walk in all the ways I command you, that it may go well with you*** (Jeremiah 7:23)**. As special agents in training to serve God, it's important that we know and obey God's commands.**

Ruler

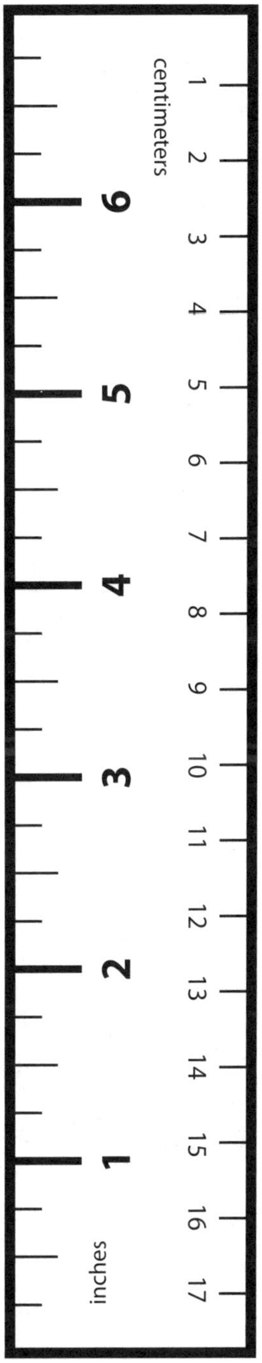

World Map

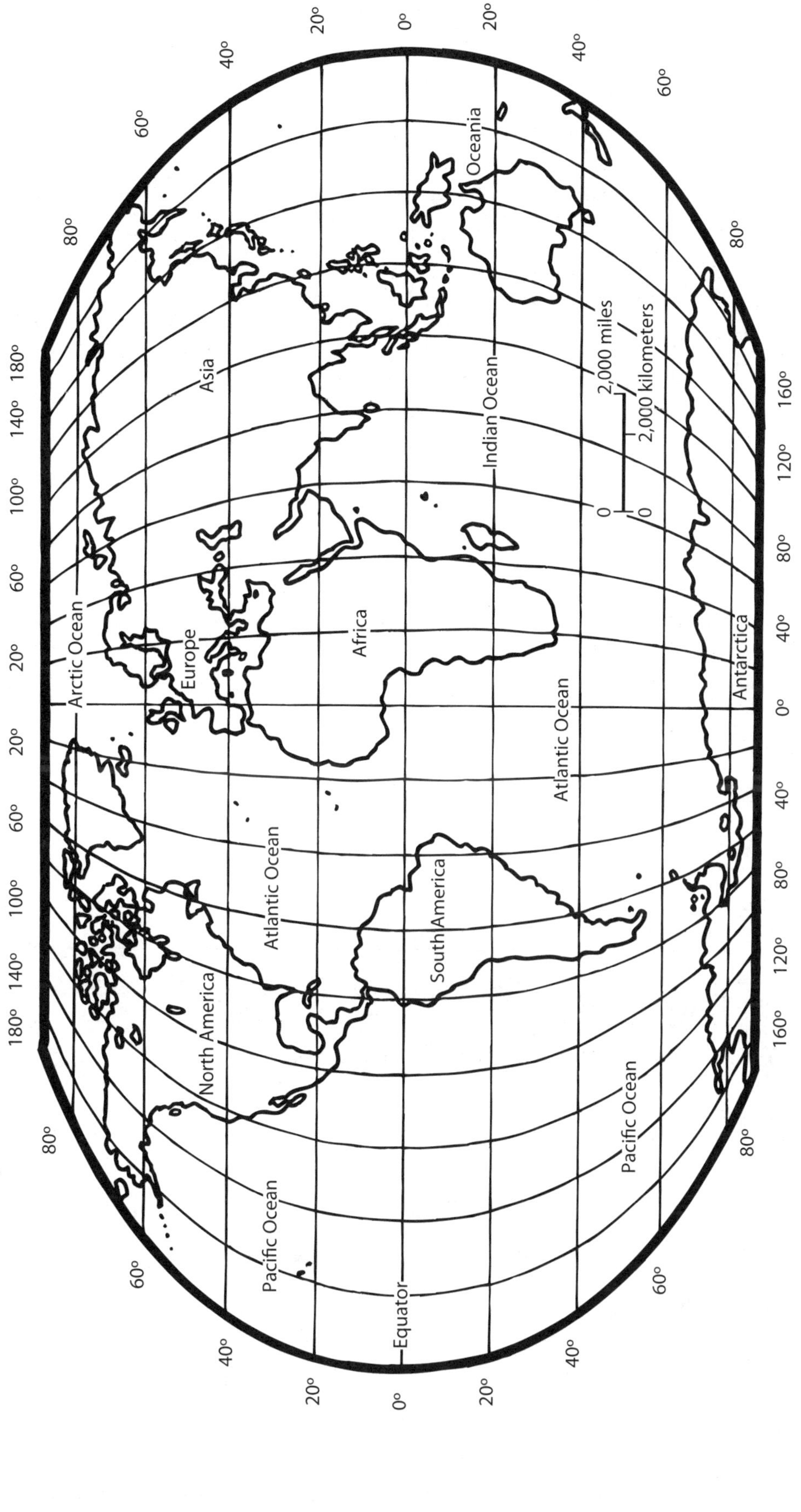

2007

JANUARY

Su	Mn	Tu	Wd	Th	Fr	Sa
	1	2	3	4	5	6
7	8	9	10	11	12	13
14	15	16	17	18	19	20
21	22	23	24	25	26	27
28	29	30	31			

FEBRUARY

Su	Mn	Tu	Wd	Th	Fr	Sa
				1	2	3
4	5	6	7	8	9	10
11	12	13	14	15	16	17
18	19	20	21	22	23	24
25	26	27	28			

MARCH

Su	Mn	Tu	Wd	Th	Fr	Sa
				1	2	3
4	5	6	7	8	9	10
11	12	13	14	15	16	17
18	19	20	21	22	23	24
25	26	27	28	29	30	31

APRIL

Su	Mn	Tu	Wd	Th	Fr	Sa
1	2	3	4	5	6	7
8	9	10	11	12	13	14
15	16	17	18	19	20	21
22	23	24	25	26	27	28
29	30					

MAY

Su	Mn	Tu	Wd	Th	Fr	Sa
		1	2	3	4	5
6	7	8	9	10	11	12
13	14	15	16	17	18	19
20	21	22	23	24	25	26
27	28	29	30	31		

JUNE

Su	Mn	Tu	Wd	Th	Fr	Sa
					1	2
3	4	5	6	7	8	9
10	11	12	13	14	15	16
17	18	19	20	21	22	23
24	25	26	27	28	29	30

JULY

Su	Mn	Tu	Wd	Th	Fr	Sa
1	2	3	4	5	6	7
8	9	10	11	12	13	14
15	16	17	18	19	20	21
22	23	24	25	26	27	28
29	30	31				

AUGUST

Su	Mn	Tu	Wd	Th	Fr	Sa
			1	2	3	4
5	6	7	8	9	10	11
12	13	14	15	16	17	18
19	20	21	22	23	24	25
26	27	28	29	30	31	

SEPTEMBER

Su	Mn	Tu	Wd	Th	Fr	Sa
						1
2	3	4	5	6	7	8
9	10	11	12	13	14	15
16	17	18	19	20	21	22
23	24	25	26	27	28	29
30						

OCTOBER

Su	Mn	Tu	Wd	Th	Fr	Sa
	1	2	3	4	5	6
7	8	9	10	11	12	13
14	15	16	17	18	19	20
21	22	23	24	25	26	27
28	29	30	31			

NOVEMBER

Su	Mn	Tu	Wd	Th	Fr	Sa
				1	2	3
4	5	6	7	8	9	10
11	12	13	14	15	16	17
18	19	20	21	22	23	24
25	26	27	28	29	30	

DECEMBER

Su	Mn	Tu	Wd	Th	Fr	Sa
						1
2	3	4	5	6	7	8
9	10	11	12	13	14	15
16	17	18	19	20	21	22
23	24	25	26	27	28	29
30	31					

2008

JANUARY

Su	Mn	Tu	Wd	Th	Fr	Sa
		1	2	3	4	5
6	7	8	9	10	11	12
13	14	15	16	17	18	19
20	21	22	23	24	25	26
27	28	29	30	31		

FEBRUARY

Su	Mn	Tu	Wd	Th	Fr	Sa
					1	2
3	4	5	6	7	8	9
10	11	12	13	14	15	16
17	18	19	20	21	22	23
24	25	26	27	28	29	

MARCH

Su	Mn	Tu	Wd	Th	Fr	Sa
						1
2	3	4	5	6	7	8
9	10	11	12	13	14	15
16	17	18	19	20	21	22
23	24	25	26	27	28	29
30	31					

APRIL

Su	Mn	Tu	Wd	Th	Fr	Sa
		1	2	3	4	5
6	7	8	9	10	11	12
13	14	15	16	17	18	19
20	21	22	23	24	25	26
27	28	29	30			

MAY

Su	Mn	Tu	Wd	Th	Fr	Sa
				1	2	3
4	5	6	7	8	9	10
11	12	13	14	15	16	17
18	19	20	21	22	23	24
25	26	27	28	29	30	31

JUNE

Su	Mn	Tu	Wd	Th	Fr	Sa
1	2	3	4	5	6	7
8	9	10	11	12	13	14
15	16	17	18	19	20	21
22	23	24	25	26	27	28
29	30					

JULY

Su	Mn	Tu	Wd	Th	Fr	Sa
		1	2	3	4	5
6	7	8	9	10	11	12
13	14	15	16	17	18	19
20	21	22	23	24	25	26
27	28	29	30	31		

AUGUST

Su	Mn	Tu	Wd	Th	Fr	Sa
					1	2
3	4	5	6	7	8	9
10	11	12	13	14	15	16
17	18	19	20	21	22	23
24	25	26	27	28	29	30
31						

SEPTEMBER

Su	Mn	Tu	Wd	Th	Fr	Sa
	1	2	3	4	5	6
7	8	9	10	11	12	13
14	15	16	17	18	19	20
21	22	23	24	25	26	27
28	29	30				

OCTOBER

Su	Mn	Tu	Wd	Th	Fr	Sa
			1	2	3	4
5	6	7	8	9	10	11
12	13	14	15	16	17	18
19	20	21	22	23	24	25
26	27	28	29	30	31	

NOVEMBER

Su	Mn	Tu	Wd	Th	Fr	Sa
						1
2	3	4	5	6	7	8
9	10	11	12	13	14	15
16	17	18	19	20	21	22
23	24	25	26	27	28	29
30						

DECEMBER

Su	Mn	Tu	Wd	Th	Fr	Sa
	1	2	3	4	5	6
7	8	9	10	11	12	13
14	15	16	17	18	19	20
21	22	23	24	25	26	27
28	29	30	31			

Emergency Information Card

Name: ____________________

Date of Birth: ____________________

Allergies: ____________________

Address: ____________________

Phone Number: ____________________

In case of emergency, call: ____________________

Quick Language Guide

	Spanish	French	German	Pig Latin
Hello	Hola (OH-lah)	Bonjour (bohn-ZHOOR)	Hallo	Ellohay (eh-LOW-hay)
Goodbye	Adiós (ah-dee-OHS)	Au revoir (oh-ruh-VWAR)	Auf wiedersehen (OWF VEE-dehr-zayn)	Oodbyegay (uhd-BIE-gay)
Yes	Sí (SEE)	Oui (WEE)	Ja (YAH)	Esyay (EHS-yay)
No	No (NOH)	Non (NOH)	Nein (NIEN)	Onay (OH-nay)
Please	Por favor (POHR fah-VOHR)	S'il vous plaît (See Voo PLAY)	Bitte (bih-TUH)	Easeplay (EEZ-play)
Thank you	Gracias (GRAH-see-uhs)	Merci (mehr-SEE)	Danke (DAHN-kuh)	Ankthay ouyay (AYNK-thay OO-yay)
Help!	Ayuda me! (ah-YOO-duh MAY)	Au secours! (oh-SKUR)	Hilfe! (HIHL-fuh)	Elphay! (EHLP-hay)

Survival Tips for Special Agent Missions:

1. Tell someone where you are going.
2. Never go alone, if possible.
3. Always carry enough food and water to last for two days.
4. Carry a compass and a map.
5. Wear proper equipment and clothing.
6. Carry a first-aid kit.
7. Carry a small flashlight in case it gets dark before you are rescued.
8. Carry a whistle to help rescuers locate you.
9. Carry a pencil and waterproof paper so that you can leave messages if needed.
10. Carry a small mirror so that you can signal passing planes or ships when necessary.
11. Carry a survival blanket that can be used for warmth. It can also be placed over a frame made from sticks to provide shelter.
12. Carry an ink pen with five feet of duct tape wrapped around it. This will provide quick repairs when needed.
13. Carry resealable gallon-sized bags so that you can have an instant canteen for water and to store other items when needed.
14. Carry a sewing kit for quick clothing repairs.
15. Carry your Bible! It makes for great reading.

Time Zone Gadget (20-25 MINUTES)

Materials

- Map Pattern (p. 79)
- Time Tube Pattern (p. 80)
- Base Pattern (p. 78)

Standard Supplies

- card stock
- colored pencils
- scissors
- glue sticks
- transparent tape

Preparation

Photocopy onto copier paper one Map Pattern for each child. Photocopy onto card stock one Time Tube Pattern and one Base Pattern for each child.

Conversation

Time zones were created in the late 1800s. Until then, each country measured time in its own way. Time zones became more important as it became easier to travel to different parts of the world. Your Time Zone Gadget can help you remember God's promise that no matter where you go in the world, God is with you. Joshua 1:9 says, *Be strong and courageous. Do not be terrified; do not be discouraged, for the Lord your God will be with you wherever you go.* What other promises does God give us in the Bible? (God will love us, no matter what. When we're sorry for doing something wrong, He will forgive us. He will never give up on us.)

Instruct each child in the following procedures:

- Color and cut out all patterns.
- Roll Time Tube into a cylinder and glue ends together where indicated on pattern (sketch a). Place small pieces of transparent tape along glued edge to secure.
- Line up tabs on Time Tube to match time designations on Base Pattern. Glue tabs to base and then use small pieces of transparent tape to secure (sketch b).
- Roll Map Pattern into a cylinder shape and glue ends together where indicated on pattern (sketch c). Place small pieces of transparent tape along glued edge to secure.
- Slide the Map Pattern onto the Time Tube (sketch d). Align arrows on map to match the current time at your location. Check to find the time in a city you would like to visit.

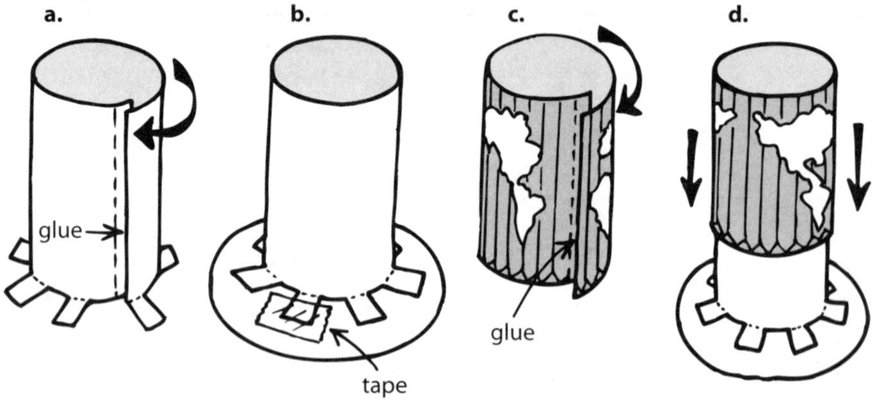

Base Pattern

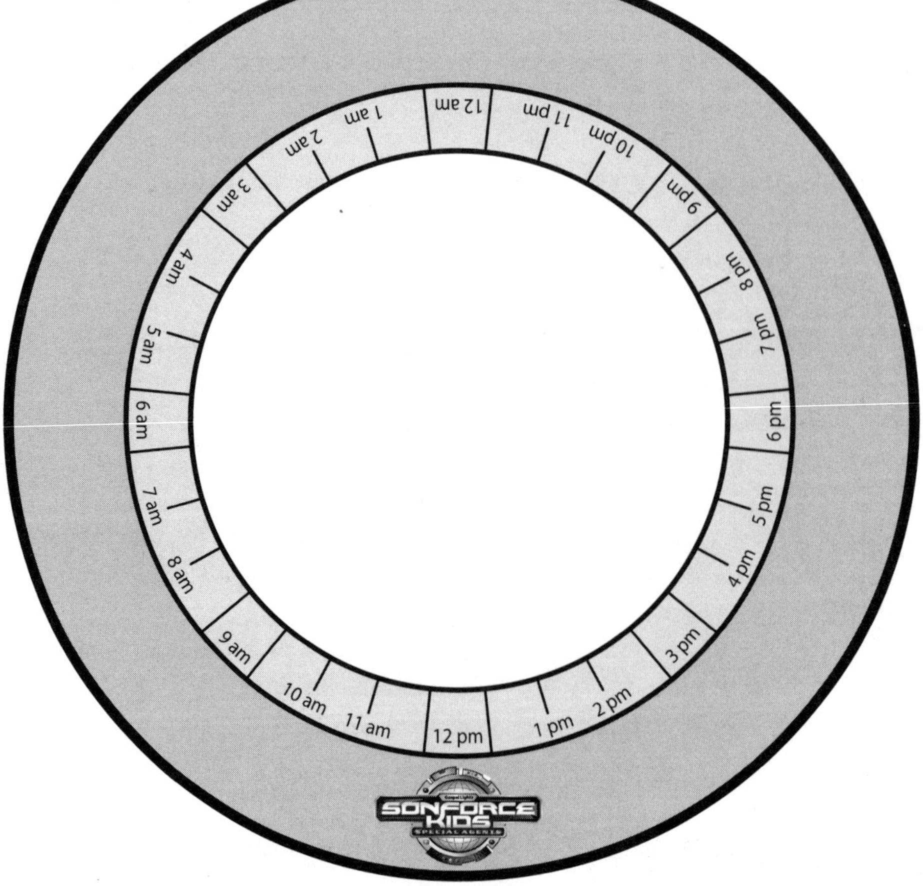

Map Pattern

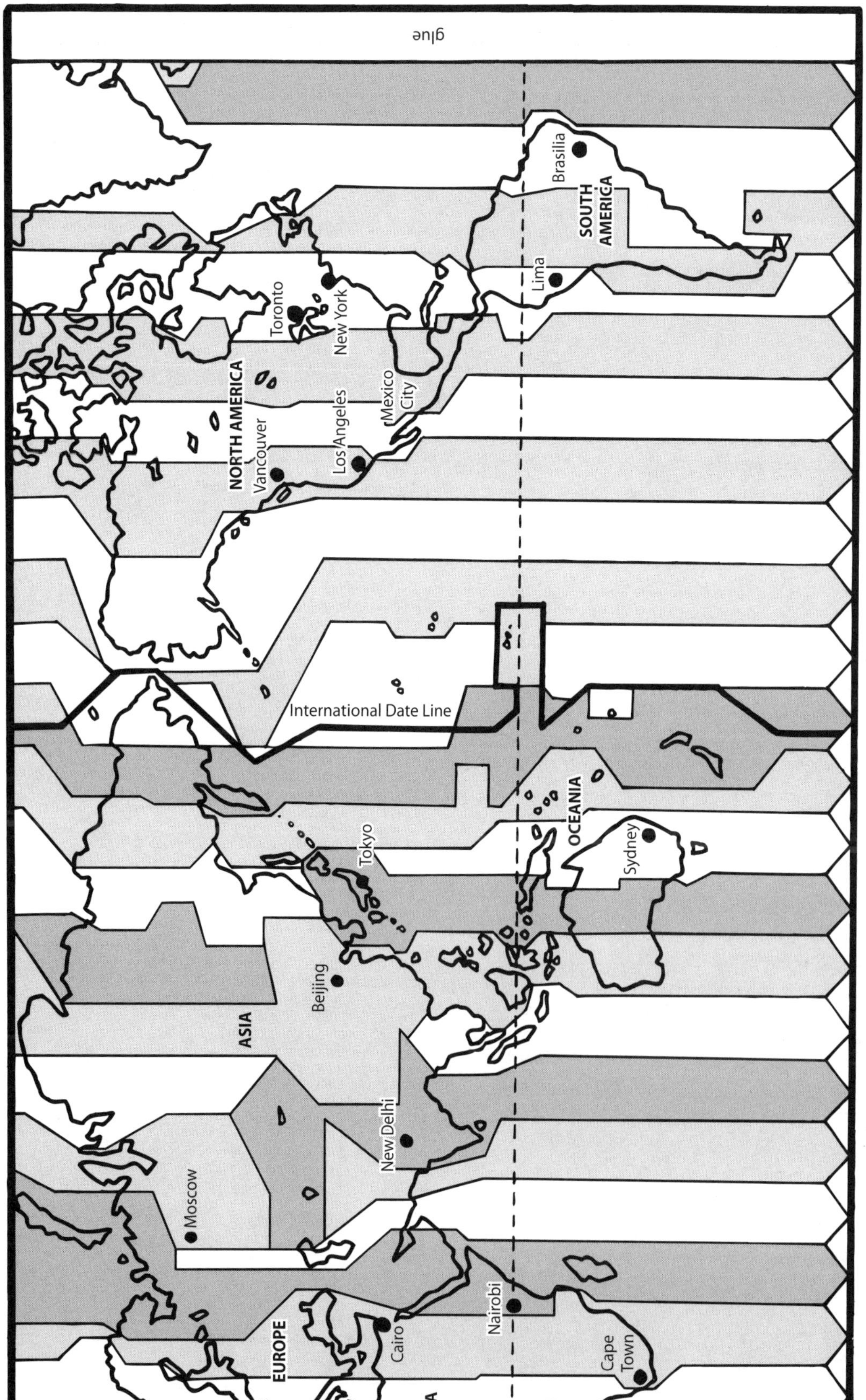
glue
SOUTH AMERICA
Brasilia
Lima
NORTH AMERICA
Toronto
New York
Vancouver
Los Angeles
Mexico City
International Date Line
OCEANIA
Sydney
ASIA
Tokyo
Beijing
New Delhi
Moscow
EUROPE
London
Paris
AFRICA
Cairo
Nairobi
Cape Town

Time Tube Pattern

Eye-See Can (20-25 MINUTES)

Materials

- old magazines

For each child—

- scissors
- empty, clean frozen juice can
- pencil with star pattern

Standard Supplies

- newspaper
- glue
- shallow containers
- paintbrushes

Preparation

Cover work area with newspaper. Pour glue into shallow containers and dilute with a small amount of water.

Conversation

Your Eye-See Can will help you remember to "keep an eye out" for ways to serve God and others. Queen Esther had to be very courageous when she went to see the king without being invited. That's why she asked God's people to unite and pray with her. God wants us to look for ways to help other people. He wants us to join with others—or "unite" with them—so that we can have courage to help the same way that Esther did. What is a way that you can serve God here at VBS, Dylan?

Instruct each child in the following procedures:

- Cut pictures of eyes (people or animal) from magazines.
- Brush a thin layer of glue over a section of juice can.
- Glue pictures to can overlapping edges (sketch a).
- Continue gluing pictures to can until it is completely covered with pictures of eyes (sketch b).
- Brush another layer of glue over entire can. Let dry.
- Place star pencil in your can. At home, fill can with pencils, pens, markers, etc. and put on your desk or dresser.

Enrichment Idea

Provide paper and markers. Children write or illustrate ways that they can serve God or others.

a.

b.

Space-Rock Secret Safe
(20–25 MINUTES)

Materials

- craft foam in various colors
- aquarium rocks in several colors
- shredded Mylar
- permanent markers in various colors
- facial tissues

For each child—

- paper-towel tube
- small plastic peanut butter jar and lid, label removed
- several small stones

Standard Supplies

- scissors
- pencils
- rulers
- craft glue

Preparation

Cut tubes into lengths equal to the depths of jars when tubes are placed inside.

Conversation

What things might you hide in your secret safe? Who do know that you could trust well enough to share the location of your secret safe with? Jeremiah 17:7 says, *Blessed is the man who trusts in the Lord, whose confidence is in him.* Trusting in the Lord means believing in the promises that He gives us in the Bible. Trusting God can give us the courage to face any situation.

Instruct each child in the following procedures:

- Place end of tube on a piece of craft foam. Draw a circle around outside of tube, about ¼ inch (.6 cm) away from edge of tube. Cut out circle.
- Squeeze glue around edge of one end of tube. Place foam circle on glued end of tube (sketch b). Set aside to dry.
- Trace around the peanut butter jar lid on a piece of craft foam. Cut out circle.
- Glue foam circle to top of lid (sketch c). Trim if needed to fit the top of lid.
- Cut out small foam shapes in contrasting colors and glue to lid to decorate.
- Lay jar on its side and fill with a layer of aquarium rocks about ½-inch (1.3-cm) deep (sketch d). Center the tube inside the jar, making sure the foam end is resting against the bottom of the jar.
- Carefully set jar upright, holding the tube in place. Allow the rocks to fill in around the tube to keep the tube upright (sketch e).
- Gently stuff tissues inside the tube to keep rocks from falling in while filling the jar.
- Carefully fill jar to the top with rocks and Mylar shreds. You may want to layer rocks of different colors.
- Squeeze a thick layer of glue over the top of rocks to keep from spilling when removing items from your safe. Let dry.
- Remove tissues from tube. Screw lid onto jar.
- Use markers to label specific rocks or rock layers as if from Mars, Neptune, the Moon, etc.
- Fill tube with small treasures. The tube should be completely concealed. No one will know that your space-rock collection is really your secret safe!

Enrichment Idea

Use beads, gears, washers, metal nuts and bolts, etc. instead of aquarium rocks.

Fabulous Flying Discs

(20-25 MINUTES)

Materials

- Shape Patterns (p. 84)
- self-adhesive craft foam in various colors
- fine-tip permanent markers in various colors

For each child—

- three discarded CDs

Standard Supplies

- card stock
- scissors
- pencils

Preparation

Photocopy one set of Shape Patterns onto card stock for every three children. Cut shapes apart, but don't cut them out.

Conversation

Ariana, you wrote "Train" on your disc. When you train to do something, you practice doing it over and over again. It's the same when you train to serve God. What are some things you can practice doing over and over when you train to serve God? (Memorize the Bible verses. Go to church so that I can learn more about God. Look for ways to help others so that I recognize when someone needs help.) **Training to serve God helps us make wise choices.**

Instruct each child in the following procedures:

- Trace a CD onto craft foam and cut out to make three foam circles. Stick one foam circle onto the label side of each CD.
- Cut out Shape Patterns. Trace patterns onto foam and cut out.
- Stick foam shapes over hole on shiny side of each CD as shown in sketch.
- Use permanent markers to write SonForce Daily Missions on CDs. (Trust. Unite. Train. Follow. Lead.)

Enrichment Idea

Decorate a sheet of foam core to make a tossing game for flying discs. Cut several 3x8-inch (7.5x20.5-cm) slots in foam core. Designate a question and point amount for each slot (see Enrichment sketch). Children take turns answering questions and trying to throw discs through slots to accumulate as many points as possible. (Optional: Divide class into teams. Each team member tries to toss his or her discs through slots. The team with most points wins.)

Enrichment

Shape Patterns

Spacewalk T-Shirt (20-25 MINUTES)

Materials

- waxed paper
- two coordinating bright, neon-colored or glow-in-the-dark fabric paints
- sponges
- fabric and glitter paints in various colors
- child-sized boots or sneakers with interesting tread patterns

For each child—

- piece of lightweight cardboard to fit inside shirt
- black or dark-blue T-shirt

Optional—

- stencil plastic

Standard Supplies

- shallow containers
- foam paintbrushes
- scissors
- ruler
- newspaper
- glue

Preparation

Cover one side of cardboard with waxed paper. Slide board inside shirt, waxed-paper side under the front of the shirt. Pour small amount of each color of paint into separate shallow containers. Cut sponges into one 1-inch (2.5-cm) square for each child. Cover work area with newspaper.

Conversation

Reading our Bible helps us know what God wants us to do to follow His path. Jeremiah 7:23 says, *Obey me, and I will be your God and you will be my people. Walk in all the ways I command you, that it may go well with you.* What are some choices you have to make to follow and obey God?

Instruct each child in the following procedures:

- Dip sponges into paint. Dab onto front of shirt to make a painted background (sketch a).
- Use a contrasting color of fabric paint to write the words "Follow God" over painted background (sketch b).
- Use foam paintbrush to paint a thin layer on bottom of boot with desired paint color. Stamp bottom of boot onto front of shirt around letters. Repeat two or three times to make shoe prints (sketch b).
- Use paint to add dots, stars, splatters and details to words and shoeprints. Let dry.

Simplification Idea

Use light-colored shirts. Write words "Follow God" with permanent markers on shirts before stamping shoe prints.

Enrichment Idea

Children paint the bottoms of their bare feet and carefully step around words "Follow God" on shirt. (Make sure to do this outdoors. Be prepared with buckets of water and towels for children to step into and wash feet immediately when finished.)

Create-a-Bot (25-35 MINUTES)

Materials

Some or all of the following—

- Styrofoam balls
- large and small Styrofoam and/or paper cups
- toilet-paper tubes
- large and small CDs
- aluminum foil
- metallic card stock or poster board
- small craft supplies (metallic chenille wires and pom-poms, wiggle eyes, buttons, etc.)
- small hardware parts (gears, washers, nuts, springs, screws, bolts, etc.)
- small office supplies (paper clips, brads, rubber bands, etc.)
- permanent markers in various colors
- wire
- silver duct tape
- colored electrical tape

Standard Supplies

- boxes or plastic storage bins
- shallow containers
- scissors
- rulers
- permanent markers
- craft glue
- wire cutters

Preparation

Sort materials into individual boxes, bins or shallow containers. Place all supplies within easy reach of work area.

Instruct each child in the following procedures:

- Look through available materials. Choose items to create your own unique robot. (Refer to sketches for ideas.)
- Use glue, wire and tape to assemble robots.

Budget Tips

This is a great way to use up assorted parts left over from other projects! Ask for donations of small hardware and other random parts.

Conversation

What choices do you need to think about as you build your robot? (What materials to use. The best way to attach pieces together. What tasks the robot might be designed to do.) **Everything you do requires making choices. Listening to each other's ideas can help you find a solution for making your arms or attaching a head. The Bible says, *Listen to advice and accept instruction, and in the end you will be wise*** (Proverbs 19:20). **Who are some people that you can ask for advice when you have a problem, Amanda? It's wise to talk to your mom when you need help with something.**

Courage Magnets (20-25 MINUTES)

Materials

- Magnet Patterns (p. 87)
- fine-tip permanent markers in various colors
- silicone glue (available in hardware stores)

For each child—

- three ¾-inch (1.9-cm) button magnets
- three 1-inch (2.5-cm), clear, flat marbles (available in floral section of craft stores)

Optional—

- toothpicks

Standard Supplies

- card stock
- scissors

Preparation

Photocopy one set of Magnet Patterns onto card stock for each child.

Conversation

Queen Esther showed love and honor for her people even at the risk of her life. When is a time you can stand up for a friend? Romans 12:10 says, *Be devoted to one another in brotherly love. Honor one another above yourselves.* Your magnets will remind you that you can have courage to stand up for others, too.

Instruct each child in the following procedures:

- Use permanent markers to color Magnet Patterns.
- Cut out patterns.
- Lay magnets on table. Squeeze a chocolate-chip-sized dot of silicone glue in the center of one magnet (sketch a). Be sure glue is on the non-attracting side of the magnet.
- Place one pattern, picture-side-up on magnet and press to spread glue evenly between picture and magnet (sketch a).
- Squeeze a second chocolate-chip-sized dot of silicone glue in the center of picture.
- Press the flat side of a marble onto dot of glue to spread glue over the surface of picture, attaching marble to picture and magnet (sketch b). Avoid skin contact with silicone glue. (Optional: Use a toothpick, rather than fingers, to press edge of picture to marble.) Let dry completely.
- Repeat process with two remaining magnets.

Enrichment Idea

Children design their own pictures to glue between marbles and magnets. Or they use small magazine pictures, first gluing them to white paper to keep dark color of magnet from showing through.

a.

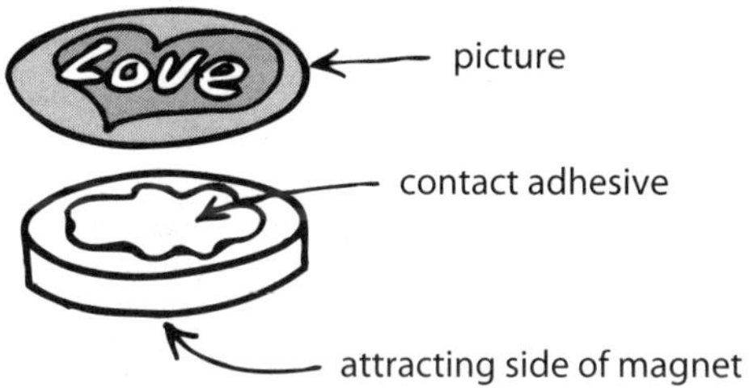

b.

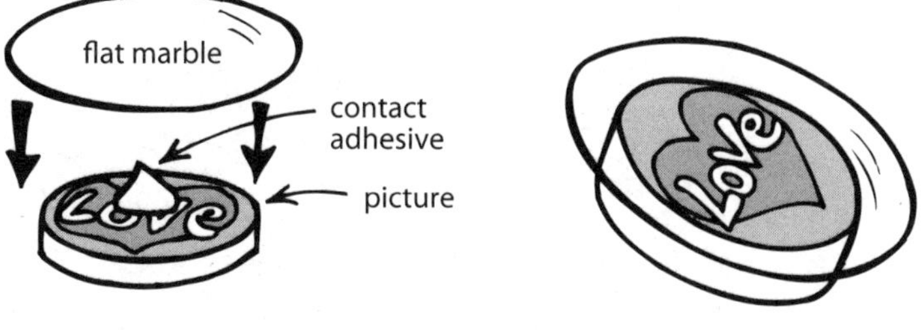

Magnet Patterns

Mission Patches (20-25 MINUTES)

Materials

- Patch Patterns (p. 89)
- self-adhesive felt in various light colors
- fine-tip permanent markers in various colors
- brightly colored fabric paint in squeeze bottles
- glow-in-the-dark paint in squeeze bottles

Standard Supplies

- card stock
- pencils
- scissors

Preparation

Photocopy one set of Patch Patterns onto card stock for every four to six children.

Instruct each child in the following procedures:

- Choose a Patch Pattern and trace around it onto self-adhesive felt. Cut out.
- Design on felt shape a patch illustrating one Daily Mission: "Trust," "Unite," "Train," "Follow" and "Lead." (Note: Refer to Patch Patterns for design ideas.)
- Sketch with a pencil and then use permanent markers to outline design on felt shape.
- Add details around words with paint (dots, outlines, stars, squiggles) as shown in sketch. Let dry.
- At home, stick your patch on a piece of clothing, backpack, book cover, etc.

Conversation

Moses' family trusted in God's love when they put Moses in a basket in the river. Miriam showed courage by staying nearby to watch and see what happened to Moses. What is a way that you can trust in God's plans for your life? When might trusting in God's love for you help you have courage? The Bible says, *Blessed is the man who trusts in the Lord, whose confidence is in him* (Jeremiah 17:7)**. God wants us to know that we can trust Him in every situation.**

God's
Trust
Plans

TRAIN
4 GOD'S SERVICE

GOD'S
Follow
PATH

Wise Words Bookmark (25-30 MINUTES)

Materials

- Bookmark Patterns (p. 91)
- card stock in various colors
- neon-colored copier paper
- paper cutter
- fine-tip permanent markers in various colors

For each child—

- two bright-colored rubber bands

Standard Supplies

- scissors
- ruler
- hole punches

Preparation

Photocopy Bookmark Patterns onto colored card stock, making several of each color for children to choose from. Cut colored paper into seven 1x8½-inch (2.5x21.5-cm) strips for each child. (Note: Be prepared to demonstrate how to fold paper for bookmark by practicing several times before children arrive.)

Conversation

Proverbs 19:20 says, *Listen to advice and accept instruction, and in the end you will be wise.* Where can we find advice and instruction from God? (In the Bible.) **What are some wise choices you can make at home? At school? When you read your Bible and do what it says, you will learn to make wise choices. Your bookmark will remind you to read God's Word every day.**

Instruct each child in the following procedures:

- Fold each strip of paper as shown in sketch a.
- Weave strips together to form a zig-zag chain, as shown in sketch b.
- Choose and cut out two Bookmark Patterns.
- Use markers to write "Proverbs 19:20" on one shape and "Train for God's Service" on the other.
- Punch a hole at the top of each pattern. Loop and secure a rubber band through each hole (sketch c).
- Punch a hole at each end of zig-zag chain. Loop and secure one rubber band with pattern to each end of chain (sketch d).

Enrichment Ideas

Children write Bible verses or references directly onto woven strips. Add stickers for more colorful decorations.

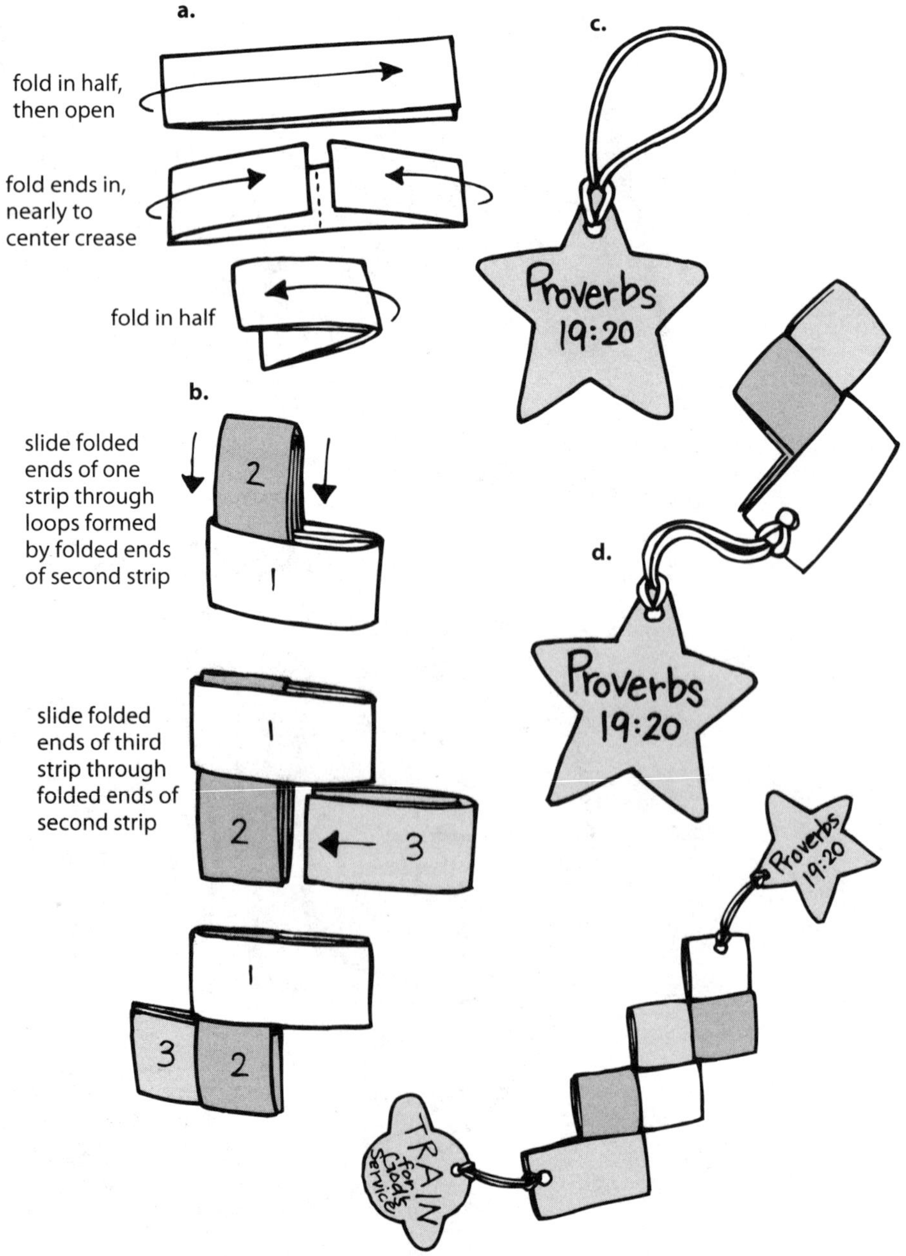

Bookmark Patterns

God's Promises Keychain (25-30 MINUTES)

Materials

- Promise Patterns (p. 93)
- drill with $\frac{3}{16}$-inch (4-mm) bit
- card stock in various colors
- self-adhesive craft foam sheets in various colors
- yarn
- pony beads
- acrylic gemstones
- sequins
- fine-tip permanent markers in various colors
- glitter glue pens

For each child—

- breath-mint tin with lid
- key ring (see sketches)

Standard Supplies

- scissors
- ruler
- shallow containers
- hole punch

Preparation

Drill a hole in the side of breath-mint tin (sketch a). Photocopy one set of Promise Patterns onto colored card stock for each child. Cut some of foam into 4-inch (10-cm) scraps. Cut yarn into one 8-inch (20.5-cm) length for each child. Pour pony beads, acrylic gemstones and sequins into shallow containers.

Conversation

Your God's Promises Keychains will help you remember some of the promises God has given us in the Bible. Which one is your favorite promise, Samuel?

Instruct each child in the following procedures:

- Trace around top and bottom of breath-mint tin onto craft foam (sketch b). Cut out shapes and stick to top and bottom of tin.
- Use permanent markers to write "God's Promises" on top of tin.
- Cut small shapes from foam scraps. Use hole punch to punch out small circles. Peel and stick shapes to top and bottom of tin (sketch c).
- Use glitter glue pens to add details and designs.
- Decorate with glitter glue, acrylic gemstones and sequins.
- Tie yarn through ring on keychain so that knot is in the center of the yarn.
- Thread several beads onto both ends of yarn (sketch d).
- Thread both ends of yarn through the lid in tin so that ends are inside tin.
- Thread a bead onto one end of yarn. Knot ends of yarn together and trim ends (sketch e).
- Cut out Promise Patterns and place inside tin.

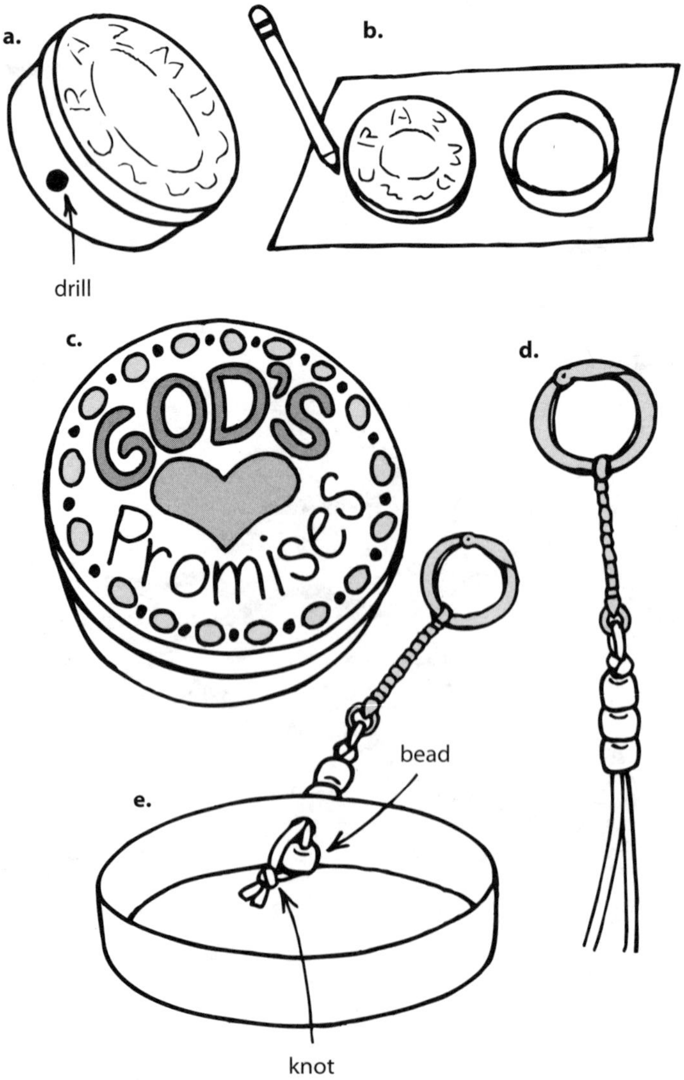

Promise Patterns

"Blessed is the man who trusts in the Lord, whose confidence is in him."
Jeremiah 17:7

"Be devoted to one another in brotherly love. Honor one another above yourselves."
Romans 12:10

"Listen to advice and accept instruction, and in the end you will be wise."
Proverbs 19:20

"Obey me, and I will be your God and you will be my people. Walk in all the ways I command you, that it may go well with you."
Jeremiah 7:23

"Be strong and courageous. Do not be terrified; do not be discouraged, for the Lord your God will be with you wherever you go."
Joshua 1:19

Starry Night Pillow

(TWO-DAY CRAFT/40-50 MINUTES TOTAL TIME)

Materials

- Star Pattern (p. 95)
- 11x17-inch (28x43-cm) copier paper
- squeeze fabric paint in metallic colors
- several pairs of fabric scissors
- straight pins
- stamps with space theme
- acrylic paints in metallic colors
- embroidery floss in metallic colors
- embroidery needles

For every three or four children—

- ½ yard (45.5 cm) of black polar fleece or felt
- 15 to 20 oz. of fiberfill stuffing

Standard Supplies

- lightweight cardboard
- markers
- scissors
- craft glue or fabric glue
- shallow containers
- paper towels
- rulers

Conversation

I saw many of you helping each other with your Star Pillows. Some things are easier to do when you have help from a friend. The Bible tells us to *Be devoted to one another in brotherly love. Honor one another above yourselves* (Romans 12:10). When you help your friends, you are doing what the Bible tells you to do in Romans 12:10. You are honoring one another above yourself. What are some things that it's easier to do when you work together?

DAY ONE Preparation

Use photocopier to enlarge Star Pattern onto 11x17-inch (28x43-cm) paper, making pattern as large as possible. Trace photocopied pattern onto cardboard to make one pattern for each child and cut out. Fold each piece of fabric in half; cut through both layers to make folded rectangles slightly larger than the pattern that will be placed on them (to make more manageable for children and to reduce waste). Pour paint into shallow containers. Place paper towels next to paint.

Instruct each child in the following procedures:

- Lay Star Pattern on two layers of fabric and trace around pattern with a marker (sketch a). Remove pattern.
- Place several pins along inside edge of line to hold fabric layers together. Use fabric scissors to cut out shape (sketch b).
- Keeping fabric pinned together, carefully squeeze a SOLID line of glue between edges of fabric, leaving about a 4-inch (10-cm) opening at top of star (sketch c).
- Press edges together firmly.
- Decorate pillow with stamps and fabric paint if desired. Press stamp into paint and gently push down onto fabric. (Note: If needed, press stamp onto paper towel before pressing onto fabric to remove excess paint.) Use fabric paints to add details such as lines, dots and squiggles. Or paint the word "SonForce" on pillow (sketch d).
- Allow glue and paint to dry overnight.

DAY TWO Preparation

Instruct each child in the following procedures:

- Remove pins from pillow.
- Stuff stars with fiberfill. Use a ruler to push it deep into pillow.
- Cut a length of embroidery floss about 18 inches (45.5 cm) long. Thread floss through a needle and knot one end.
- Sew a running stitch through all layers to close pillow opening (sketch e). Knot end of floss and pull through pillow to hide it inside. Trim ends.

Simplification Idea

Make this craft in one day by machine-stitching pillow pieces together before class time. Children stuff and finish as directed.

a.

b.

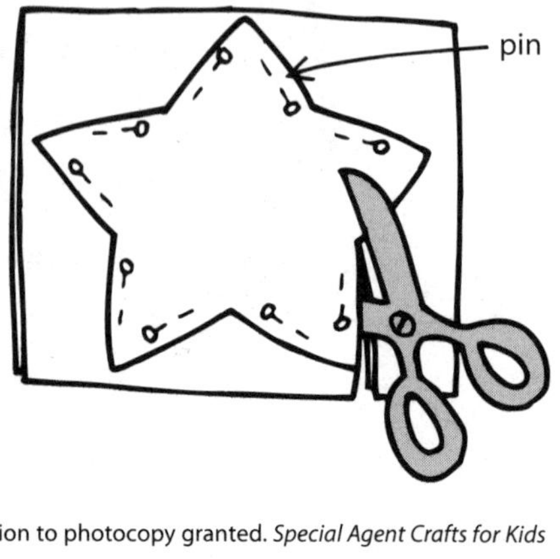

c.

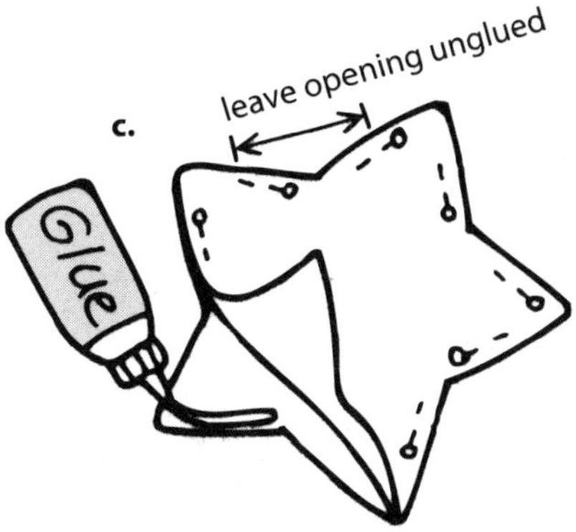

d.

e.

Star Pattern

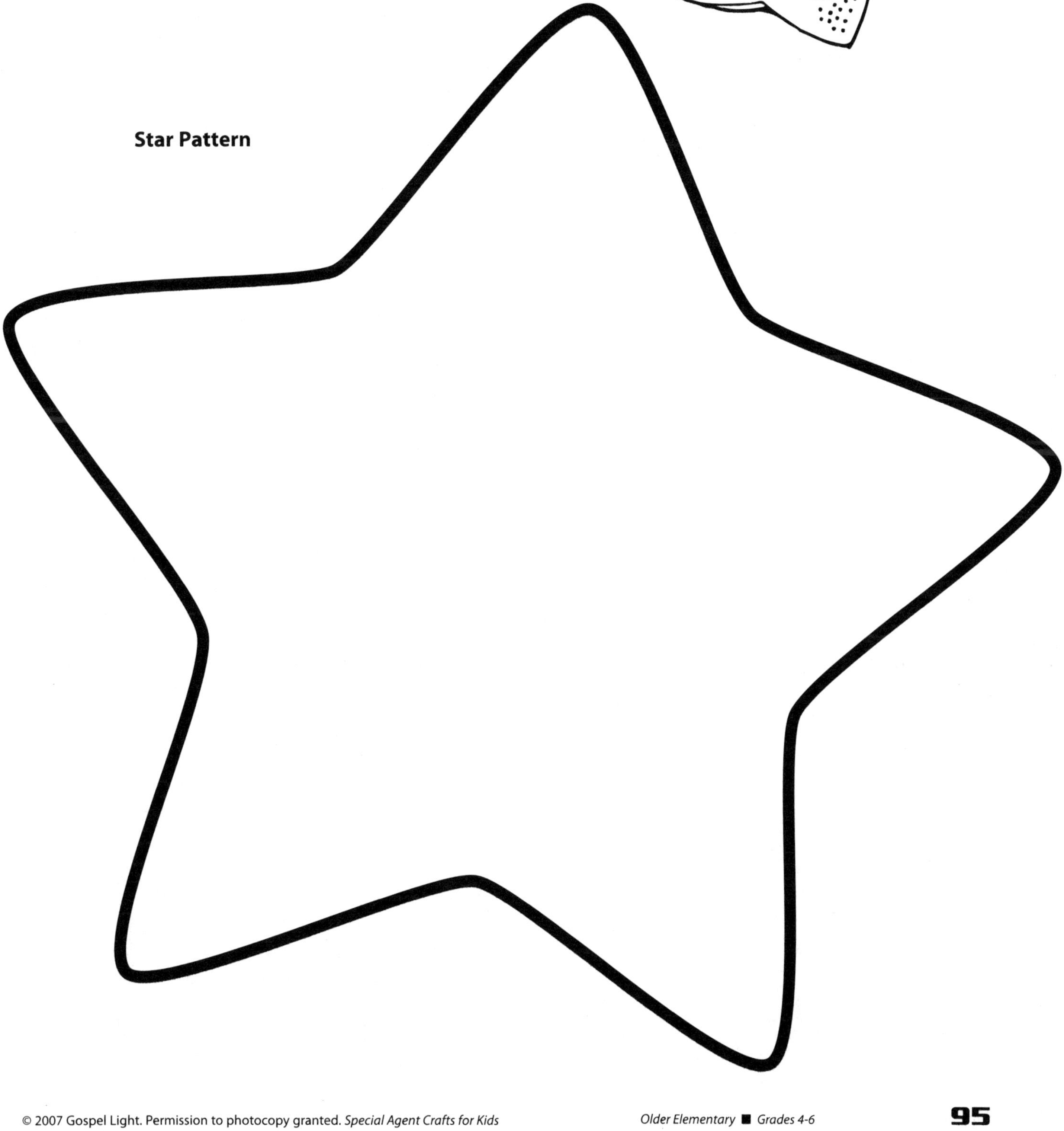

Index of Crafts